"Govindarajan is a master of taking the complicated and making it simple. Do not underestimate the power of the three-box model. It applies universally to businesses small and mega. A common language within an organization can mean the difference between success and failure. Read this and incorporate it into your DNA. You will be a winner."

—**BILL ACHTMEYER,** founder, Parthenon; Senior Managing Director, Parthenon-EY

"As in Govindarajan's other books that I have read, *The Three-Box Solution* takes what can be a complex set of issues and simplifies them into a very crisp and thorough thought process. It provides a sound framework for thinking about how your organization is doing and whether you are taking the necessary steps to ensure relevancy in the future. This book is worth reading more than once; I highly recommend it."

—**SAMUEL R. ALLEN,** Chairman and CEO, Deere & Company

"Interesting read! The examples provide a practical view on how companies have utilized three-box thinking, focusing on the core while creating the future through linear and nonlinear innovation. This concept has influenced my thinking and approach to augmenting the core of our business and investing in the future."

—**MAHESH AMALEAN,** Chairman and cofounder, MAS Holdings

"*The Three-Box Solution* is a simple, elegant, yet powerful way of addressing the future. While the book codifies practices from successful examples, it is the ambition and passion of the leader to grow despite challenges that provide the horsepower for change. As the book beautifully brings out, the passionate leader does not wait for a crisis to create the future. It is part of his or her daily management discipline."

—**T. K. BALAJI,** Managing Director, Lucas-TVS Limited

"*The Three-Box Solution* offers a deeply practical and instructive framework to help businesses confront one of the key challenges in the global marketplace: how to innovate and grow in a sustained way. Drawing on more than thirty years of teaching, writing, and consulting, Govindarajan provides a winning combination of strategic insights and actionable steps designed to help virtually any business or organization build a better future."

—**AJAY BANGA,** President and CEO, MasterCard Inc.

"It is very refreshing to read *The Three-Box Solution* because of both its relevance and its simplicity. As you read the book, you connect with events in your own journey as you grapple simultaneously with ideas such as learning from the past, living in the present, and dreaming about the future. The simplicity of Govindarajan's model, like all great ideas, triggers you to think, 'Hey, why did I not think about it this way?' I recommend this book and its approach to both current and aspiring CEOs. Business schools will also find this approach worthy of teaching, and chief strategy officers will find it most useful."

—**BHASKAR BHAT,** CEO, Titan Watch

"CEOs and boards increasingly struggle with the need to be ready for the future and yet to 'perform while you transform.' At last, there is a road map that gives concrete terms for how to do this systematically and successfully."

—**RAMA BIJAPURKAR,** bestselling author; management consultant; and board member

"*The Three-Box Solution* brilliantly tackles the challenges of a successful company to continually drive the linear innovation essential for today's operational excellence, while nurturing the nonlinear innovation necessary to create the company's future. In describing how to escape the insidious traps of the past, the book clearly articulates how companies can leverage today's strengths while building the capabilities needed to execute their vision for the future.

Govindarajan's thirty years of passion and experience effectively help us identify the leadership behaviors, processes, and metrics that companies seeking to adopt balanced Three-Box Solutions need, and how this approach can create the change-ready culture required for sustainable leadership in rapidly evolving industries.

As the leader of a very successful company that operates in a rapidly changing marketplace, I will be able to leverage many of the three-box balance principles as I drive our future agenda."

—**GIOVANNI CAFORIO,** CEO, Bristol-Myers Squibb

"*The Three-Box Solution* is essential reading for any senior executive leading a successful company with a proud history. Govindarajan gives a clear path for how to create the environment and culture within a company to foster innovation that will make a difference in ensuring a bright future for an organization.

Govindarajan trains our senior executives at Thermo Fisher Scientific; our teams practice what he preaches."

—**MARC CASPER,** President and CEO, Thermo Fisher Scientific Inc.

"In *The Three-Box Solution*, Govindarajan offers a compelling framework for driving innovation while delivering current goals, without the constraints of past successes and failures. With powerful, international examples, he offers a clear guide to creating the sustainable, innovation culture needed to stay ahead."

—IAN COOK, Chairman, President, and CEO, Colgate-Palmolive Company

"At Thinkers50, we are passionate about the very best in management thinking. Govindarajan is a Thinkers50 Award winner and one of our highest-ranked business thinkers. *The Three-Box Solution* proves why: important ideas, accessibly presented, and practical."

—STUART CRAINER and DES DEARLOVE, founders, Thinkers50

"What a compelling piece of work—and its genius is in its simplicity. Leaders at all levels of the organization should find the three-box model for innovation a how-to manual for success."

—ALEXANDER M. CUTLER, Chairman and CEO, Eaton Corporation

"*The Three-Box Solution* is an extremely stimulating, encouraging, valuable, and enjoyable read.

I've spent more than a decade leading and shaping organizations using a systemic, 'future-back' approach to drive performance today and consciously choosing what from the past serves the future (and what doesn't). Govindarajan brings to life so many real examples of how other organizations are using this approach, framing it in the context of the simple, but hugely powerful three-box model. I was struck by the Hindu roots of the thinking, which added huge power and validity to the model.

The book's structure is also very helpful, with a few focused chapters and rich, highly relevant case studies bringing the key points to life in a practical and vivid way. The takeaways at the ends of chapters were extremely valuable, focusing the whole work on real-life application rather than theoretical strategy."

—STUART FLETCHER, CEO, Bupa

"Adequately balancing today's urgencies with tomorrow's challenges is at the heart of every company's mission. However, we all know that accomplishing this goal is easier said than done. *The Three-Box Solution* offers a simple but powerful framework guiding leaders to act swiftly and thoughtfully in the present while remaining vigilant regarding the challenges of the future. It offers pragmatic tools to help companies make those hard choices necessary to deliver sustainable results."

    —RODRIGO CALVO GALINDO, President and CEO, Kroton Educacional

"Leaders must continuously attend to Box 1, Box 2, and Box 3. Govindarajan offers a simple but powerful framework to achieve three-box balance. Managers at all levels within the Godrej Group will find his ideas extremely valuable."

    —ADI GODREJ, Chairman, Godrej Industries

"The unprecedented pace of change in today's business environment necessitates nimble, brave, frame-breaking thinking to ensure significant and enduring success. A longtime mentor to Hasbro, Govindarajan offers a simple yet profound Three-Box Solution that has inspired our teams to create a culture of innovation, challenge the trappings of the past, and create our future. In *The Three-Box Solution*, Govindarajan concisely and bravely distills key insights applicable across varied industries and provides practical takeaways to facilitate execution. The book is a must-read for any manager who values courageous leadership, adaptability, and foresight."

    —BRIAN D. GOLDNER, Chairman, President, and CEO, Hasbro, Inc.

"If your company needs to stop doing what it's done and branch out in new and profitable ways, this is the book for you."

    —MARSHALL GOLDSMITH, *New York Times* and *Wall Street Journal* bestselling author, *Triggers*

"Govindarajan introduced the Three-Box Solution to GE a few years ago when he was our professor in residence at Crotonville. We embraced it immediately because we saw in it a path to strategic fitness and innovation that was simple, powerful, and purposeful. Rich in research, storytelling, and perspectives from the field, the book will be a provocative and practical guide for those who have to build new muscle memory as they adapt and optimize for today while preparing to win in the future."

    —JEFFREY R. IMMELT, Chairman and CEO, General Electric Company

"The three-box approach is not only an excellent read but a superb guidance manual for anyone formulating and driving a long-term company strategy. The book is written in a simple, highly readable style with valuable and interesting examples of real-world corporate experiences. At the end of each chapter is a critical analysis of the key elements in the preceding section, with probing questions and discussion of trade-offs. The book, an excellent resource for managers and leaders at all levels, forces one to think hard about how to develop and execute a long-term business strategy that will deliver sustainable success."

— **OMAR ISHRAK,** Chairman and CEO, Medtronic

"The three-box framework is powerful. The first box lulls you, the second is excruciatingly difficult, and most of us do not get to see the third—it's too late. While the status quo appears to be the easiest solution, Govindarajan uses examples—from sports to Hindu mythology—to inject three-box thinking into the organizational DNA. The book is a true primer for a nonlinear business world riddled with discontinuities and constant change, where you slide to irrelevance in a blink. It makes you think, think, think! And execute."

— **K. V. KAMATH,** President, New Development Bank BRICS; former Chairman and CEO, ICICI Bank

"Exquisitely simple and compelling, this book represents a unique and important contribution by providing a framework that drives leaders to balance the delivery of results for today with creating value for tomorrow."

— **RESHMA KEWALRAMANI,** MD, FASN, Vice President and head, U.S. Medical Organization, Amgen Inc.

"The automotive industry is changing faster than ever. At Visteon, we're transforming our business for sustainable success in this evolving landscape. The framework suggested in *The Three-Box Solution* is very useful as a guide for balancing the demands of current performance while building the future at the same time. A must-read for any CEOs who are facing the challenge of transforming their business."

— **SACHIN LAWANDE,** President and CEO, Visteon Corporation

"The elegant simplicity of Govindarajan's Three-Box Solution provides a framework for enabling the Mahindra Group to balance the imperatives of the present with the demands of the future. It is a construct that permeates all our strategic thinking."

— **ANAND G. MAHINDRA,** Chairman and Managing Director, Mahindra Group

"Govindarajan has the rare ability to filter out complexity to help leaders focus on the most salient issues. At its core, strategy is about the choices needed to establish a winning position. Too many organizations approach strategy in ways that magnify the periphery, obscure the fundamental choices, and paralyze breakthrough thinking. In *The Three-Box Solution*, Govindarajan distills the choices organizations must make to ensure long-term success into clear categories that will help build strategic alignment at all levels. Govindarajan's second box crystallizes the unappreciated strategic principle that success depends on what you choose not to do. Letting go is what enables you to move forward. Organizations that embrace the Three-Box Solution will optimize the allocation of resources to leverage today's success factors while building the innovative platform for a long-term winning position."

—JOHN McCLELLAN, Managing Director, Thought Leadership, Palladium

"*The Three-Box Solution* offers a fresh perspective and actionable framework that leaders can use to create a culture of operational excellence, continuous improvement, and innovation within their organizations. Using credible, real-world examples, Govindarajan illustrates the three-box model's effectiveness in helping leaders balance short-term business demands with long-term innovation and growth goals. This book is a must-read for leaders who want a simple, intuitive approach to unlocking innovation within their organization and achieving sustained long-term competitive advantage in their business."

—JONATHAN E. MICHAEL, Chairman, President, and CEO, RLI Corporation

"Govindarajan offers unique insights into the need to balance the demands of the present with those of the future. He highlights the importance of investing wisely in building the future while creating a sense of urgency about embracing change. Many managers will relate to the caution he urges about getting too caught up in the all-consuming demands of the present. For a more-than-century-old organization like Tata, his three-box framework offers many important lessons."

—CYRUS MISTRY, Chairman, Tata Group

"In today's world, organizations need to continuously innovate and demonstrate a high degree of learnability to stay relevant and ahead of the competition. Through real-life cases and simple frameworks, Govindarajan provides insight and guidance on how leaders can prime organizations for the future while balancing priorities of the present. *The Three-Box Solution* is a must-read for leaders at all levels."

—NARAYANA MURTHY, cofounder, Infosys Limited

"The three-box approach is a pragmatic way to think through and balance the needs of existing business and crafting a future. Explained in a simple manner, it provides a framework that leaders can use to reflect on the dynamics of business and attain present and future goals. In today's business environment, leaders are required to run both a sprint and a marathon at the same time."

— **ABIDALI Z. NEEMUCHWALA**, CEO, Wipro Limited

"In *The Three-Box Solution*, Govindarajan articulates a highly practical framework that helps everyone in the organization balance the competing activities of running the current business while imagining and building a new one. He's taken this a step further, adding a third, often overlooked, but critical element to his model: escaping the traps of the past by abandoning practices and attitudes no longer relevant in a changed environment. At PepsiCo, we practice what Govindarajan preaches."

— **INDRA K. NOOYI**, Chairman and CEO, PepsiCo, Inc.

"*The Three-Box Solution* offers a sound, strategic approach to ensure that Caterpillar's long history of innovation—developing, designing, and manufacturing the machines and engines our customers want and need—continues."

— **DOUG OBERHELMAN**, Chairman and CEO, Caterpillar Inc.

"In his latest book, *The Three-Box Solution*, Govindarajan has defined a framework that brilliantly outlines our practices. At Harman, we strive to balance innovation (Box 3) and execution (Box 1), while shifting our mind-set from automotive supplier to technology leader (Box 2). Linear innovation provides the daily fuel to drive the corporation, while exponential innovation is the jet engine that propels a corporation to sustained profitable growth. This framework is embedded in our culture and has enabled us to deliver above-market growth for many years."

— **DINESH C. PALIWAL**, Chairman, President, and CEO, Harman International

"*The Three-Box Solution* applies a deceptively simple framework that can help lead the way to a more coherent strategy by providing both stimulating questions and tools."

— **DEEPA PRAHALAD**, innovation/design consultant; coauthor, *Predictable Magic*

"The topic of innovation can fall prey to some very tiresome treatments. Govindarajan offers a fresh perspective on innovation by introducing the concept of harmony, not just between the past, present, and future, but also between the equally important forces of creation, preservation, and destruction. Don't limit your application of *The Three-Box Solution* to your business. Apply it to your life."

—**DHIRAJ RAJARAM,** founder, CEO, and Chairman, Mu Sigma Inc.

"This thoughtful book is a must-read for leaders and managers in today's fast-changing and hypercompetitive world. *The Three-Box Solution* teaches how it is possible to successfully manage the present while systematically building for the future."

—**CARLOS RODRIGUEZ-PASTOR,** CEO and Chairman, Interbank

"'Unanswered questions' are better than 'unquestioned answers.' *The Three-Box Solution* addresses both, remarkably and yet simply. A must-read for personal as well as organizational reinvention."

—**HIMANSHU SAXENA,** founder and CEO, Center of Strategic Mindset

"Govindarajan helped our entire leadership team think differently about where to spend its time, simply by outlining the importance and interrelationship of the three boxes. As he says, the more success you have in Box 1, the harder it is to devote time to Boxes 2 and 3. The three boxes have become part of the team's lexicon, and we devote real effort to balancing our time, attention, and focus.

The parable of the four monkeys is particularly enlightening. Organizational forgetting (Box 2), though indispensable, is extremely difficult.

Personally, I use Govindarajan's three-box concept as a way to challenge myself and my team. I work very hard to push myself out of the 'tranquil refuge' of Box 1 and squarely into the 'difficult and painful' work of Box 2 and the often languishing but intellectually thrilling possibilities of Box 3. I now constantly measure the amount of time my team spends on each of the three boxes and try to adjust in real time to increase our focus on the future. It is not unusual to have one of my team members call me out publicly for spending too much time in Box 1."

—**THOMAS WARSOP,** President and CEO, The Warranty Group

"*The Three-Box Solution* presents a simple, yet powerful framework to simultaneously optimize continuous process improvement and breakthrough innovation. This book will be inspiring for management executives since both operational excellence and innovation are critical for future."

—**ZHANG RUIMIN,** founder, Chairman, and CEO, Haier Group

The Three-Box Solution

Create the Future, Forget the Past, and
Manage the Present

THE

THREE

SOLUTION

BOX

A Strategy for Leading
Innovation

VIJAY GOVINDARAJAN

Harvard Business Review Press
Boston, Massachusetts

Copyright 2016 Vijay Govindarajan
All rights reserved
Printed in the United States of America

10 9 8

No part of this publication may be reproduced, stored in or introduced into a retrieval system, or transmitted, in any form, or by any means (electronic, mechanical, photocopying, recording, or otherwise), without the prior permission of the publisher. Requests for permission should be directed to permissions@hbsp.harvard.edu, or mailed to Permissions, Harvard Business School Publishing, 60 Harvard Way, Boston, Massachusetts 02163.

The web addresses referenced in this book were live and correct at the time of the book's publication but may be subject to change.

Cataloging-in-Publication data is forthcoming.

ISBN: 978-1-63369-014-1
eISBN: 978-1-63369-015-8

The paper used in this publication meets the requirements of the American National Standard for Permanence of Paper for Publications and Documents in Libraries and Archives Z39.48-1992.

To my grandfather Tagore Thatha
who invested countless hours in my education
to guide—and secure—my future.

R.T. Velu Studio, Annamalainagar, India.

Contents

1

A Simple Framework
for Leading Innovation:
The Three Boxes

Leaders already know that innovation calls for a different set of skills, metrics, methods, mind-sets, and leadership approaches: they understand that creating a new business and optimizing an already existing one are two fundamentally different management challenges. The real problem for leaders is doing both, simultaneously. How do you align your organization on the critical, but competing, behaviors and activities required to simultaneously meet the performance requirements of the current business—one that is still thriving—while dramatically reinventing it?

Managers and executives, consultants and academics, and analysts and thought leaders around the world have long wrestled with this question, and in response, some of them have developed a concept known as "ambidexterity": an organizational capability of fulfilling both managerial imperatives at once.[1]

But what's missing is a simple and practical way for managers to allocate their—and their organization's—time and attention and resources on a day-to-day basis across the competing demands of managing today's requirements and tomorrow's possibilities. Managers need a simple tool—a new vocabulary, if you will—for managing and measuring the different sets of skills and behaviors across all levels of the organization. They need a practical tool that explicitly recognizes—and resolves—the inherent tensions of asking people to innovate and, at the same time, to run a business.

What's more—as anyone who has tried to lead innovation knows—the challenge goes beyond being ambidextrous in order to simultaneously manage today's business while creating tomorrow's. There is a third, and even more intractable, problem: letting go of yesterday's values and beliefs that keep the company stuck in the past.

What leaders need now is the Three-Box Solution.

The Three-Box Solution

The ability to achieve significant *nonlinear* change starts with the realization that time is a continuum. The future is not located on some far-off horizon, and you cannot postpone the work of building it until tomorrow. To get to the future, you must build it day by day. That means being able to *selectively* set aside certain beliefs, assumptions, and practices created in and by the past that would otherwise become a rock wall between your business of today and its future potential. This basic idea is behind what I call the Three-Box Solution (see figure 1-1).

The Three-Box Solution is a simple framework that recognizes all three competing challenges managers face when leading innovation. It's a powerful guide for aligning organizations and teams on

FIGURE 1-1

The Three-Box Solution

By balancing the three boxes, managers can resolve the inherent tension of innovating a new business while running a high-performing business at the same time.

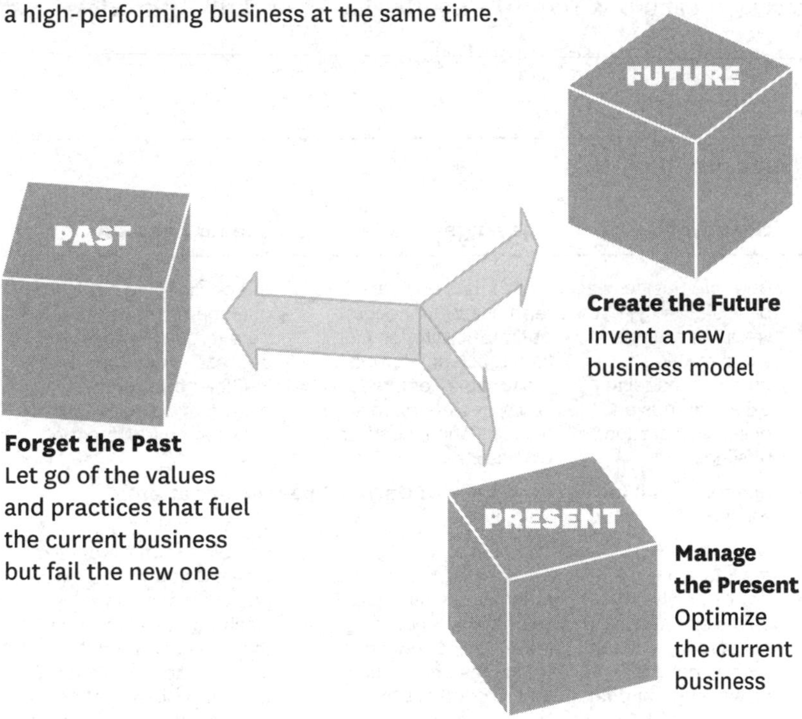

FUTURE

PAST

Create the Future
Invent a new
business model

Forget the Past
Let go of the values
and practices that fuel
the current business
but fail the new one

PRESENT

**Manage
the Present**
Optimize
the current
business

the critical but competing activities required to simultaneously create a new business while optimizing the current one. In the three boxes, companies must do the following:

- Box 1—Manage the present core business at peak efficiency and profitability.

- Box 2—Escape the traps of the past by identifying and divesting businesses and abandoning practices, ideas, and attitudes that have lost relevance in a changed environment.

- Box 3—Generate breakthrough ideas and convert them into new products and businesses.

Success in each box requires a different set of skills, attitudes, practices, and leadership (see table 1-1).

TABLE 1-1

The Three-Box Solution

	Strategy	Challenge	Leader behavior
Box 1	Run core business at peak efficiency; use linear innovations within existing business model to extend brands and/or improve product offerings.	Keep focus on near-term customer needs; optimize operations for high efficiency/lowest reasonable cost; reduce variance from plan; align rewards and incentives with strategy.	Set challenging goals for peak performance; analyze data to quickly spot and address exceptions and inefficiencies; create a culture of doing everything smarter, faster, cheaper.
	Leaders at all levels, especially CEOs, must pay regular attention to each box.		
Box 2	Ability to build the future day by day begins here; create space and supporting structure for new nonlinear ideas; let go of past practices, habits, activities, and attitudes.	The past always fights back, so be prepared to make tough calls about values Box 3 needs to leave behind (remembering that some are still useful and needed in Box 1).	Establish formal regime of planned opportunism (i.e., gathering and analyzing weak signals); champion the ideas of maverick thinkers; do not tolerate obstructionism—set an example for the enterprise by visibly and publicly penalizing foot-draggers; anticipate the need for an orderly process of experimentation.
	Just as Boxes 2 and 3 must be protected, Box 1 must remain focused and undistracted.		
Box 3	The nonlinear future is built mainly by experimentation that tests assumptions and resolves uncertainties, hedging risk; new learning either strengthens an idea or reveals its weaknesses.	It's not always obvious which ideas to pursue first—you need a method to gauge relative value and priority; expand variance, knowing success rate in Box 3 experiments is low; do not trim sails on Box 3 projects in a downturn.	Measure progress of Box 3 efforts not on revenue development but on the quality and pace of learning from experiments; since many nonlinear ideas launch into embryonic markets, it's important to test assumptions not only about the product but also the business model and the developing market.
	With the three boxes kept in balance, a business can change dynamically over time.		

By balancing the activities and behaviors associated with each box, every day, your organization will be inventing the future as a steady process over time rather than as a onetime, cataclysmic, do-or-die event. Simply put, the future is shaped by what you do, and don't do, today.

What You Will Get from This Book

I have developed the Three-Box Solution over the course of thirty-five years of working with and doing research in corporations worldwide. It is the foundation of my thinking and teaching about strategy and innovation. In presenting the three-box framework to students and executives, I have been gratified to see how strongly it resonates with people. Business leaders from all kinds of organizations, such as GE, Tata Consultancy Services, Keurig Coffee, IBM, and Mahindra & Mahindra, who are featured in this book have told me they value the simplicity and clarity of the framework. But even more, they recognize that these ideas have the power to solve complex and intransigent business problems. As Beth Comstock, who serves as the president and CEO of GE Business Innovations and GE's chief marketing officer (CMO), told me:

> *The three-box framework allowed General Electric to develop processes around our "protected class" of ideas that are given more time and space to prove their worth after they pass through an initial stage of rigorous testing. This "pivot-or-persevere" mind-set has allowed us to function more as a start-up and given rise to products such as the Durathon battery, which we took from lab to market in five years. Along with helping to set and align our portfolio, the three-box framework led us to think of innovation as a process. It's the way we're evolving the company and becoming faster, simpler, and more inventive.*

Her colleague, Raghu Krishnamoorthy, the vice president of human resources at GE Crotonville, echoes these themes, emphasizing the lasting impact of the ideas on the company:

The three-box framework gave our business teams the opportunity to reflect, debate, and establish the strategic center of gravity in both short and long terms. And it sparked new conversations within the organization relative to where energy and resources should be spent to achieve the best balance in managing "the current" while creating "the future." The approach proved to be effective across the company as leaders recognized a more powerful correlation between quantum improvements and quantum change and made a lasting impact in expanding our views, strengthening our culture, and positioning our organization for continued growth.

My aim in writing the book is to provide insight and guidance that will help you and your organization attend to the long-term future with the same commitment and consistency with which you are driven to act on the clamorous priorities of the present. My hope is that the Three-Box Solution will make your job of leading innovation easier, with a simple vocabulary and set of tools that you can cascade down and across your organization, as GE has done.

The Three-Box Solution describes and illustrates, with in-depth examples, the framework for building the future *continuously* instead of waiting for the next crisis or for a new competitor to come out of the blue with a brilliant future you never imagined. The book is meant for leaders at all levels—from the small team to the functional department, from the business unit to the corner office, from managers responsible for the daily execution of the core business to those who drive and inspire innovation. The more people in a company who understand how the three boxes work, the better prepared that organization will be to anticipate and exploit changes of all kinds—to act instead of react. The Three-Box Solution framework has the potential to transform the future of any organization that embraces it, whether it's a large, for-profit enterprise; a midsize business; or a small nonprofit institution.

Let's turn to the story of one of those organizations.

Transforming Hasbro

In the mid-1990s, toy giant Hasbro saw itself as a product company. Its offerings consisted mainly of toys (among them G.I. Joe, Transformers, and My Little Pony) and board games (The Game of Life, Monopoly, Candy Land, and Chutes and Ladders). Hasbro competed in an industry broadly referred to as "family entertainment"—toys and games described by marketers as appealing to "kids from two to ninety-two." Until the 1990s, people typically purchased Hasbro products in a retail store. Customers shopped, bought, and returned home with a toy or game.

Today, Hasbro is very different; it's a self-styled "branded-play company." Its relationships with customers may or may not begin with a physical product on a physical shelf. Instead, the Hasbro universe features numerous constellations serving as points of entry. Customers get to know and use Hasbro's core brands across multiple platforms: online games and fan sites, movies and television shows, digital gaming systems, and comic books and magazines produced through partnerships with Disney and other companies. The goal is to create many opportunities for ongoing exposure to, and experience of, the various Hasbro brands. Hasbro has parlayed the popular Transformers line, for example, into a wide array of media, products, and experiences. (See the sidebar, "Transformers' Metamorphosis into a Lifestyle Brand.")

Transformers' Metamorphosis into a Lifestyle Brand

Hasbro's line of Transformers toys and action figures is aptly named. Since the creatively changeable products debuted in 1984, they've morphed into an ever-expanding array of branded manifestations beyond the toys themselves:

- Universal Studios Hollywood, Transformers: The Ride-3D (you must be at least forty inches tall)

- Movies and television shows

- Clothing (T-shirts, jackets, hoodies) in infant, child, and adult sizes

- Character costumes, including helmets, masks, armor, and weaponry

- Backpacks and lunch bags

- Games for Xbox and PlayStation console systems

- Room décor, including Transformers-themed comforters, sheets, pillowcases, and wall decals (be sure to get Mom's permission first)

- Print and digital comic books (through an arrangement with IDW Publishing)

Many of Hasbro's other brands have also pursued this kind of ubiquitous experiential marketing strategy—lifestyle brands that have a 360-degree impact and influence on consumers. While families might once have played

---

For Hasbro, the differences between the past and now are dramatic. Yet, over the years during which I have closely observed this company, I have been struck by the fact that the changes were not sudden but were the result of continuing attention, experimentation, and learning—some of it ambiguous or inconclusive—that spanned most

board games together on rainy days or in the evening, today they can wear branded Transformers clothing, go to Transformers movies, travel to theme parks to experience a 3D Transformers ride, or decorate their children's rooms with Transformers bedding. The Box 3 strategy is to create and capture value from the brand across multiple platforms.

Source: Photos copyright TRANSFORMERS® and copyright 2015 Hasbro, Inc. Used with permission.

of two decades. For Hasbro, inventing the future was more of a steady process than a cataclysmic event.

The story of Hasbro's transformation neatly showcases the themes at the heart of this book: how organizations can, in a balanced way, *manage their present core businesses at peak efficiency and profitability*

(Box 1); *escape the insidious traps of the past* (Box 2); and *innovate nonlinear futures* (Box 3).

Why Is It So Hard to Balance the Three Boxes?

For a long time, I have been troubled to see how often organizations fail to invest wisely in their futures while instead placing dominant emphasis on the present. To be sure, the Box 1 present is vitally important. Box 1 is the *performance engine*. It both funds day-to-day operations and generates profits for the future. Where problems arise is when the present crowds out other strategic priorities—for example, when the *only* skills brought into a business are those that serve today's core.

That is shortsighted in every sense of the word. As Box 1 grows in dominance, Box 3 languishes and Box 2 barely exists. This is a tragic waste. Businesses achieve strategic fitness only when they thoroughly understand and carefully manage the benefits and risks of each of the three boxes. The three-box framework will help you deliver stronger overall performance and more-innovative futures while also building an organization fit to survive not just from quarter to quarter but for generations. As Karim Tabbouche, the chief strategy officer of VIVA Bahrain, told me: "Our planning process had become myopic and short term in nature, with our objectives becoming tactical and linear in nature. The three-box framework has challenged us to redesign the planning process, which would allow us to brainstorm Box 2 and Box 3 nonlinear initiatives in addition to undertaking Box 1 operational excellence initiatives. It is important to allocate resources to Box 1, Box 2, and Box 3 projects to maintain a healthy balance among the boxes."

Yet it is not surprising that so many organizations focus mainly— even exclusively—on Box 1. The Box 1 present is their comfort zone, based on activities and ideas that are proven, well understood, and firmly embedded in the business. Most firms' organizational structures were built on the successes of the past, refined over time to support the priorities of the present core business, and focused on maximizing cash flow and profit generated by the core.

By comparison, the Box 2 work of avoiding the traps of the past is difficult and painful. It may require wrenching management decisions to divest long-standing lines of business or to abandon entrenched practices and attitudes that are unwelcoming or even hostile to ideas that don't conform to the dominant model of past success. Moreover, the Box 3 methodology for creating the future consists of leaps of faith and experimentation that are fraught with uncertainty and risk. The regime calls for entirely different management strategies and metrics than does the relatively settled and predictable work of executing the present core business at the highest level.

So Box 1 is, by contrast, a tranquil refuge:

- The rewards of focusing on the present are immediate, easy to forecast, and easy to measure. Markets apply continuous pressure on businesses to maximize present opportunities and opposing pressure to steer clear of nebulous long-term distractions.

- The skills and expertise needed to thrive in the present are known and abundantly available, whereas ten to fifteen years out is a black box. Every bet you place on the future is an exercise in brain-cramping guesswork. And the results likely won't be known for a long time to come.

- The risks of the present are relatively low. Those that exist— market volatility, macroeconomic forces, competitors' moves, and regulatory and political changes—are generally well understood and manageable through established means.

- Even though the long-term risks of neglecting the future are immense, they are too distant and abstract to provoke a sense of motivating urgency.

Yet a sense of urgency is exactly what's needed. To become disproportionately devoted to Box 1 is to leave vital organizational muscles underdeveloped; when you suddenly need them in a pinch, they won't be ready. The only sane recourse is to exercise all of the organization's muscle groups regularly, just as you would to keep yourself physically fit. The three boxes, managed together and given the requisite ongoing attention, achieve a level of balance that in the long run helps organizations avoid self-inflicted crises and respond opportunistically to the unavoidable ones.

One of the things you will discover, once you begin to pay daily attention to each of the three boxes, is that they are interrelated and indispensable to each other. I like the way Hasbro CEO Brian Goldner describes them: "For me, the three boxes are like a Russian nesting doll. They are doppelgangers that are influenced by the shape and size of the others and can't be dealt with separately."

Another thing you will discover is that although they are interrelated, the three boxes call for divergent skills, disciplines, and management strategies. Leaders therefore need to become more than *ambidextrous*, as I mentioned earlier, as they transition among the boxes. Because it is so easy to default to Box 1, spreading attention around to all three will require conscious discipline. Hasbro's Goldner logs the amount of time he devotes to each box: "I quite literally review my calendar every week to make sure I'm allocating enough attention to Boxes 2 and 3."

The goal of achieving balance among the three boxes requires understanding that each box defines success in its particular context:

- The skills and experience you apply in Box 1 allow you to *operate at peak efficiency and execute linear innovations in your core businesses.*

- The skills of Box 2 allow you to *selectively forget the past* by identifying and divesting businesses and abandoning practices, ideas, and attitudes that have lost relevance in a changed environment and would otherwise interfere with your focus on inventing the future.

- The skills of Box 3 allow you to *generate nonlinear ideas and convert them, through experimentation, into new products and business models.*

Ultimately, the Three-Box Solution is about managing the natural tension among the values of *preservation, destruction,* and *creation*—forces with which I was abundantly familiar growing up in India. (See the sidebar, "The Hindu Roots of the Three-Box Solution," for a glimpse into my framework's philosophical underpinnings.)

The Success Trap

The biggest challenge you have in balancing the three boxes is that the greater your success in Box 1, the more difficulties you are likely to face in conceiving and executing breakthrough Box 3 strategies. This "success trap" typically arises not from willful inattention but from the overwhelming power of success that the past has brought.

The most pernicious effect of the success trap is that it encourages a business to suppose it already knows what it needs to know in order to succeed in the future. But that's not true. Organizations that do not continuously learn new things will die.

Like most other forms of popular entertainment, Hasbro competes in a "hits-based" industry, launching many new products in the hope that one or more will become the sort of breakout platform or franchise that vastly overcompensates for the cost of developing products that don't hit it big. Over the years, Hasbro has had its share of

The Hindu Roots of the Three-Box Solution

In the Hindu faith, the three main gods are Vishnu, Shiva, and Brahma. Vishnu is the god of preservation, Shiva is the god of destruction, and Brahma is the god of creation. This triumvirate of familiar Hindu deities corresponds to the work of sustaining a thriving business. Like Vishnu, the firm must preserve its existing core; like Shiva, it must destroy unproductive vestiges of the past; and like Brahma, it must create a potent new future that will replenish what time and circumstance have destroyed.

Hindu myth makers paired each of the three gods with symbolically relevant wives. Vishnu's wife is Lakshmi, who bestows wealth, just as Box 1 produces current profits. Shiva's partner is Parvathi, who symbolizes power, a vital Box 2 necessity when selectively destroying the past. Brahma is betrothed to Saraswathi, who symbolizes creativity and knowledge—the critical inputs for Box 3 innovations and the wellspring of future profits.

According to Hindu philosophy, creation-preservation-destruction is a continuous cycle without a beginning or an end. Each of the three gods plays an equally important role in creating and maintaining all forms of life. Further, Hinduism states that while changes in the universe can be quite dramatic, the processes leading to those changes usually are evolutionary, involving many smaller steps. Consistent with this philosophy, the work of sustaining an enterprise is a dynamic and rhythmic process, one that never ends.

I have never before encountered an organization that has encoded the Three-Box Solution into its organizational scheme as explicitly as Mu Sigma, a rapidly growing decision sciences and big data analytics firm with

legendary hits (Mr. Potato Head, G.I. Joe, and Transformers), each becoming a growth platform. But until twenty years ago, the company had continued to see itself as a toy and game manufacturer for the retail channel.

The risk for a business of Hasbro's type is that it could become complacent, resting on its laurels and perhaps failing to notice changes in the environment that could threaten a formerly secure business headquarters in Chicago and an innovation and development center in Bangalore, backed by Sequoia Capital and General Atlantic. Inspired by his grandmother's narration of stories from Hindu mythology, Mu Sigma founder and CEO Dhiraj Rajaram has used the three main deities of the Hindu faith to conceive a sustainably harmonized approach to the cycles of preservation, destruction, and creation.

The company divides its leadership into three "clans"—the Vishnu (preservation), Shiva (destruction), and Brahma (creation). On the company website, the leadership team members are explicitly designated Vishnu, Shiva, and Brahma. The designations are not arbitrary. They are based on an assessment of the natural propensities of each leader. The expectation is that having explicit roles will help the cause of harmony among the three boxes.

The three clans engage in a dynamic, cyclical process of challenge and response. According to Rajaram, "There is a contest among the clans, with each one testing the other to provoke the most rigorous defense of its plans and ideas." Vishnu challenges Shiva over what to preserve versus what to forget; Shiva challenges Brahma over which new ideas are truly worth pursuing. "Only when each intended move is explored and challenged from every angle can the best solutions emerge," said Rajaram. Creating the clans, he added, "was a way for the three-box concept to become ingrained in the company culture. It is the constant engagement of these three that helps organizations to benefit from change."

model. That is why organizations must develop the Box 2 capacity to overcome the influence of the past, to divest one identity in favor of another.

That said, one thing Hasbro has going for it is a history of executing sudden and startling mutations. Founded in the 1920s by three brothers named Hassenfeld, the company was first a textile-remnants business but soon began to manufacture pencil boxes and other school supplies. When its pencil supplier raised prices, the company began manufacturing its own pencils, a successful enterprise that lasted into the 1980s and provided profits that funded other products and ventures. Coinciding with the postwar plastics revolution of the 1940s, the company launched its earliest toys (doctor and nurse kits with play stethoscopes, thermometers, and syringes). Mr. Potato Head debuted in 1952.

Businesses less metamorphic than Hasbro may face a steeper climb to develop their Box 2 disciplines. The work of Box 1, being founded on past success, is typically structured according to the operational disciplines engendered by that success. The fruits of success are real and the demands to sustain them are constant. From this defining DNA, firms create their systems, processes, and cultures. These structures shape the way an organization approaches everything it does: how it hires, promotes, invests, measures performance, formulates strategy, and evaluates ideas and opportunities. *Linear* ideas (those that conform with the past) tend to be adopted easily, whereas *nonlinear* ideas (nonconforming and therefore both uncertain and threatening) tend to be rejected easily.

One of the practical implications is that you don't want Box 1 teams being distracted from their performance goals—and they don't want to be distracted from the goals either. The general manager of MeYou Health, Trapper Markelz, told me about the time his company tried to use the "core" sales team to sell a radically new product:

In 2014 my Box 3 dedicated team had a powerful new product. Initially, we used the [shared corporate] sales team, but it was not prioritizing our product because it targeted different customer segments at a different price point. Sales were lagging significantly behind targets. Before learning about three-box thinking, I believed this to be a training problem. After three-box thinking, I came to understand the challenge: my business unit was asking the sales team to do different (Box 3), while the rest of the company was asking them to do more (Box 1). We can't expect them to do both. So I proposed to the CEO that we fund the creation of a separate sales and marketing team for my business unit.

This is the trap that past success can engender. Ideas that differ substantially from those we are accustomed to almost always struggle to take root. As much as we might pay lip service to the fact that the future will differ dramatically from the past, we often behave as though it will be exactly the same.

Had Hasbro continued to see itself as a toy and game manufacturer whose customer relationships existed only at the retail point of sale, it would not be the successful company it is today. In the intervening decades, it transformed itself by shedding its old identities. That is among the many reasons why Box 2, whose mechanisms explicitly target success traps, is such an important enabler of Box 3 innovation. Later on you will see, in the example of United Rentals (chapter 4), that Box 2 disciplines can sometimes also be useful in helping to reconceive the way the Box 1 performance engine executes the core business.

Linear and Nonlinear Innovation

Another challenge you will have in balancing the three boxes is that Box 1 and Box 3 require distinctive forms of innovation. Leading innovation calls for fundamentally different management approaches in the two boxes. That's why it is critical to distinguish between the respective types of innovation.

There are many typologies used to classify innovation: Innovations can be sustaining or disruptive. They can be incremental or radical.

They can be competency enhancing or competency destroying. They can relate to product or process. However, I divide *all* innovations into two main types:

- *Linear* innovations improve the performance of your *current* business model. As such, they are part of the work of Box 1. For example, Hasbro developed *Star Wars*–themed versions of two of its classics: the game of Monopoly and Mr. Potato Head ("Darth Tater"). Both were brand extensions within an essentially unchanged business model. This type of innovation builds on the present core, making use of Box 1 knowledge, systems, and structures. Linear innovation is thus straightforward, unambiguous, and unthreatening to the status quo.

- *Nonlinear* innovations, the domain of Box 3, create *new* business models by dramatically (1) redefining your set of customers, (2) reinventing the value you offer them, and/or (3) redesigning the end-to-end value-chain architecture by which you deliver that value. As you will see, Hasbro executed variants of all three approaches, offering new value to new sets of customers across a dramatically redesigned value chain.

Preparing for Futures You Cannot Predict: Planned Optimism, Weak Signals, and the Daily Built Future

As the cliché asserts, "Fortune favors the well prepared." Equally true is that misfortune afflicts the unprepared. Partly because their energies are overinvested in the Box 1 present, leaders often find it difficult to remember that *the future is now*. It is built day by day, a little at a time, beginning with *what you do today that adds something new to what you did yesterday.* Karan Gupta, managing director of IE Business School, told me that using the three-box framework has had an impact there:

> *Though the three-box idea is simple, it is extremely difficult to put into practice. Getting out of one's daily activities and focusing on the future is easier said than done. However, applying the three-box model produces major impact. Constant reminders and the promise to "look in the mirror every day and ask oneself what one has done in Box 3 today" have helped our managers to excel in their daily activities and focus on the future. I noticed a remarkable change in managers. They performed their daily activities more efficiently so that they could free up time for Box 3 ideas.*

Daily investments in Box 3 activity prepare you for whatever the unknowable future brings—good or bad. Failing to make those investments will likely result in a disappointing or endangered future.

Why is it so difficult to practice this simple lesson? *Because when you neglect the future today, you don't see the damage today.*

Consider a Box 3 activity for an individual: doing regular exercise to ensure future health. Executives with hectic travel schedules commonly find it difficult to sustain an exercise routine. Everyone knows that travel can be draining. Since a single day's failure to exercise exacts what feels like only a trivial cost, it is easy to choose *not* to go to the hotel fitness room to exercise. However, the costs of this choice accumulate over time, leading to a future of declining health in the form of added pounds, greater unrelieved stress, lower energy and endurance, and perhaps the higher risk of a serious illness.

As with the failure to make ongoing investments in personal fitness, businesses that do not attend to their own futures day in and day out are likely to be surprised eventually by a crisis—one that may have been brewing for years. On the other hand, if you proactively attend to the future *every day*, you earn the opportunity to shape the future to your advantage. Businesses must develop an active innovation culture through what I call *planned opportunism*. Planned opportunism is about a set of leadership behaviors and actions that *prepares you for the futures you cannot predict*. In practice, that means building an assortment of forward-looking competencies and embracing the disciplines of experimentation that create the flexibility to both pursue and shape the unexpected opportunities that come your way. The issue is not one of predicting the future; it is about being prepared for circumstances you do not exclusively control.

Planned opportunism is one of the Three-Box Solution's most important concepts. It is a way to compensate for unpredictability of all kinds—good and bad. A simple example of this lurks in an observation that many business thinkers have made but which most organizations find difficult to put into practice: businesses that make across-the-board cuts, including cuts to strategic activities, during a downturn recover less resiliently than those that make more targeted cuts or even increase their investments in key Box 3 initiatives. In the latter case, it is planned opportunism that allows a business to deal with difficult circumstances by acting from a position of strategic confidence rather than one of fear or panic.

Institutionally, Hasbro became quite good over the years at practicing planned opportunism. I have included in table 1-2 a list of strategic discontinuities—diverse nonlinear changes relevant to Hasbro's competitive environment—that occurred during the years between the mid-1990s and 2015. How likely is it that the Hasbro of twenty years ago could have predicted all of these changes? Not very. But it would have been able to generate informed hypotheses pointing in productive directions. To do that would have required a level of insight formed in part by what futurists call "weak signals."[2]

TABLE 1-2

Twenty years of strategic shifts in family entertainment, 1995–2015

Technology	Family entertainment concepts	Retail channels	Demography	Globalization
Proprietary gaming systems/ platforms Robotics Rapid growth of internet and wireless, evolving to dominant entertainment channel Handheld digital devices and media (cameras, smartphones, tablets, etc.) Shrinking product life cycles plus rapid technology advances put intense downward price pressure on technology-based games.	Families spend less time playing together; play is thus more age segmented. Parents in two-income households spend less time with children but have more money to entertain children. Parents prefer toys and games that offer enrichment value. Many children are hyper-scheduled and have less leisure time; when they play, they are often by themselves and prefer fast-paced video games.	Big-box stores drive retail consolidation, crowding out small mom-and-pop and boutique outlets. Large retailers drive economies of scale, demand high levels of supply chain integration. Big players offer private-label products. Bankruptcy of "traditional" competitors leads to further consolidation.	Children "grow older younger," lose interest in traditional toys at an earlier age. Aging population makes grandparents a powerful buying segment; they often "own" play activities with grandkids. Adults find opportunities for play in social and/or work settings (gaming as a strategy or simulation tool). Growing minority populations soon gain majority status.	Potential growth in emerging markets, where concepts of play are different and disposable income is low. But . . . . . . in emerging markets, new approaches to product design, manufacturing, and marketing will be needed to overcome cultural, market, and logistic barriers. Thus, Western firms need to build new competencies. Growth potential in developed markets can be pursued through existing competencies.

Weak signals consist of emergent changes to technology, culture, markets, the economy, consumer tastes and behavior, and demographics. As the term suggests, weak signals are hard to evaluate because they are incomplete, unsettled, and unclear. But they are the raw material for developing hypotheses about nonlinear changes in the future. Hasbro devised a method for tapping weak signals and using them to make inferences about possible futures that might develop.

The process starts with these three basic questions:

- What particular factors and conditions does one's current success depend on?

- Which of these factors might change over time or are changing already, thus putting current success at risk?

- How can one begin to anticipate and prepare for these possible changes so as to cushion or even exploit their impact?

Having answered these questions, Hasbro over time was able to make what in retrospect were smart, nonlinear moves toward an unpredictable future. No matter what business you're in, you will benefit from being active rather than passive when dealing with time and change. That is the essence of the Three-Box Solution.

As Hasbro looked toward the future, it was able to anticipate some of the discontinuities. For example, the fact that both parents in many households held full-time jobs was already the US norm. Less clear was what that implied for the concept of family entertainment. A falling US birthrate meant Hasbro additionally faced a shrinking customer base. The company might also have seen the growing demographic diversity of its US customers. And as globalization accelerated, it might likewise have developed an appetite for the growth potential in markets around the world.

Similarly, there were weak signals even in the 1980s—the Atari video game and the personal computer revolution, for example—that gave early warning that technology would disrupt the gaming space. However, twenty years ago, there were significant unknowns about the evolution of technology-based gaming:

- How quickly would the internet become a potent channel?

- How could companies combine physical and virtual realms for their consumers?

- Who would be the new competitors in this space (Electronic Arts? Nintendo? America Online? Sony?)?

- Who might be potential new partners (Marvel Comics? Pixar?)?

- Would the PC remain the predominant platform for home technology or would a new one (mobile phones) or an old one (television) supersede it?

- What would be the new economic model when the industry moved from "analog dollars" to "digital pennies"?

Balancing the Three Boxes: Experiment to Grow Knowledge and Shrink Uncertainty

Across domains riven with uncertainty, the best way to address questions like those Hasbro faced is by conducting low-cost experiments meant to test critical unknowns en route to conceiving scalable new business models. As Goldner noted, "You must probe and learn to achieve clarity in embryonic markets." (As you will read in chapter 3, IBM's emerging business opportunities process was heavily focused on learning about technology markets so new that, like planets cooling from clouds of gas and debris, they were not yet fully formed.) In such circumstances, the experiments that arise from inferences based on weak signals must be accompanied by robust hedging strategies.

Experimentation is all about learning, but if you can't forget, you're unlikely to learn. To succeed in Box 3 creation, you must first excel in Box 2 destruction. The work of Box 2 often comes down to making key distinctions between values that are *timeless* (enduring for the long run) versus those that are *timely* (ultimately perishable with the passing of time). Think of roots and chains. If you cut a tree's roots, it dies. Therefore, leaders need to understand that their organizations' roots have timeless value and need to be preserved. Conversely, every organization also accumulates chains consisting of once-timely ideas and activities that have lost their usefulness. If you do not find and break the chains, they will keep you from getting to the future.

Organizations need to test ideas for new lines of business both for their alignment with timeless values and for the timeliness of the opportunities they present. Part of the benefit of developing a process for making such judgments lies in its capacity to help enterprises stay centered within their mission and vision.

Hasbro has never lacked for creative ideas, but one of its ventures in the 1970s offers a cautionary tale about getting ahead of oneself. In 1970, when wild adventures in diversification were in vogue across many industries, the company launched a chain of nursery schools under the Romper Room brand (made famous by a popular children's television program). There was an element of timeliness to the idea; the administration of President Richard M. Nixon had recently begun a program of child-care credits. Moreover, Hasbro believed that the schools would build on its successful line of Romper Room–branded toys. But when a product company jumps into a service business, it risks violating a timeless value and venturing out of its depth. That's where Hasbro found itself. "We'd get phone calls saying, 'We can't find one of the kids.' The whole company would stop," Alan Hassenfeld, a member of Hasbro's founding family, told the *Wall Street Journal* in a December 13, 1984, article. After five years of a bold but ill-advised strategy, Hasbro exited the nursery school business.

Not every nonlinear idea will be right for your business. Part of a sound hedging strategy when experimenting with nonlinear ideas is to assess *how far may be too far* to stretch your existing business model and internal skills. By 1970, Hasbro had settled into being primarily a maker of toys. As it considered the Romper Room nursery-school idea—notwithstanding the brand leverage it stood to gain through the schools—Hasbro could have concluded that its internal skills and culture didn't suit the demands of an early-childhood-education business model (whose degree of difficulty it may have underestimated). Getting out of the business required recognizing that the unfamiliar business model had taken Hasbro too far from its timeless center.

Balancing the Three Boxes: Structure as a Lever to Unlock New Value

"Box 2 is the most challenging in a company like Hasbro that's been around a long time," said Goldner. (See the sidebar, "Hasbro's 'Forgetting' Challenges in the Mid-1990s.")

Hasbro's "Forgetting" Challenges in the Mid-1990s

In light of the nonlinear shifts identified in table 1-2, one can speculate about several core assumptions that Hasbro needed to selectively forget to ensure future success:

- We are a product company.

- We make analog-based games that have long product life cycles, command premium prices, and generate high margins.

- We distribute through brick-and-mortar retail outlets.

- Our consumers are kids fifteen years old and younger.

- We make board games that promote face-to-face social interaction in a physical setting.

- We are an American company.

- And so on . . .

The key to a successful strategy of forgetting may turn out to require shaking things up by changing the organizational structure. Goldner remarked, "Hasbro was historically very siloed. So one of the first things we did [in the early 2000s] was move away from manufacturing categories toward a brand orientation under global brand leaders. This was a Box 2 move; we had to forget how we operated in the past." (Structural changes may sometimes be a necessary prerequisite to initiating programs of nonlinear innovation. In chapter 6, Mahindra Group CEO Anand Mahindra describes how changing the diversified company's organizational structure unleashed new market potential and a more entrepreneurial culture.)

Organizing around brand platforms gave Hasbro managers both the accountability and the authority to pursue myriad brand opportunities. And planned opportunism prepared the company to be flexible in developing strategies that could meet head-on the various changes in technology, demography, generational behavior, and global opportunity it already had identified.

In 2000, Hasbro had little presence in emerging markets. Since then, it has invested aggressively and now earns more than 50 percent of its revenues from non-US markets, including significant revenues in emerging markets. The company has increased its emphasis on digital gaming. Hasbro's global brand teams have leveraged core brands, such as Transformers, across multiple platforms: toys, movies, television, and the internet (including social media). In 2000, Hasbro's top-eight brands delivered 17 percent of total revenues; as of 2015, they accounted for more than 50 percent.

Between the end of 2000 and the first quarter of 2015, Hasbro's stock price rose from $11 to $72. This represented a compounded annual growth of 14 percent in market capitalization in fifteen years, despite the turbulence of the dot-com bust and the Great Recession. In sharp contrast, the stock price of Mattel, Hasbro's major competitor, increased from \$15 to \$25 during the same period. Even though Mattel exceeded Hasbro in sales revenue—\$6.02 billion versus \$4.3 billion in 2014—both companies had a similar market capitalization as of April 2015.

One of Hasbro's strengths is the recognition that nonlinear initiatives sometimes require rebooting. In 2009, the company eyed the growing number of cable TV networks and chose to dive in, partnering with Discovery Communications to launch The Hub Network.[3] The audience grew to roughly 70 million homes over four years. Even so, Hasbro decided to pull back from the investment in 2014, giving Discovery controlling interest in a 60/40 split. The move "incentivized [Discovery] to more fully support the network" while allowing Hasbro to "[generate] significant merchandise sales from TV shows built around *My Little Pony*, *Littlest Pet Shop*, and *Transformers Rescue Bots* that air on the channel," said Goldner.

Hasbro added to its merchandising muscle by entering into a new agreement with Disney around the same time. Disney announced it was giving Hasbro global rights to manufacture dolls from its popular Disney Princess—eleven female characters, including Cinderella, Jasmine, Mulan, and Pocahontas—and *Frozen* lines. The agreement ended Disney's nearly twenty-year relationship with Mattel and opened new horizons for Hasbro, whose target market had been tilting predominantly male. This strategic initiative leveraged Hasbro's existing resources while still taking the company in a new direction.

Goldner has initiated innovations in structure and process to keep strategic thinking sharp and ensure that continuous focus is applied to Box 3 ideas: "We have a team called Future Now that works only on the future of our brands; they don't think about how to sell the brand this year." Hasbro also considers ways the boxes can intersect and provide mutual benefit. Goldner convenes what are known as "martini meetings," so named because brainstorming at the meeting follows the shape of a martini glass. "We start at the rim, as far out as we can, and think about emerging technologies and new inventions. Real Box 3 thinking. Then we narrow these ideas down to those that are most promising. As we move closer to the stem, we see how those technologies can be applied to our current product lines."

New business structures are often indispensable to giving shape, method, and discipline to managing the boxes in concert. For both better *and* worse, organizations optimize around their core successes. It makes great sense to do so. But you must also create oases where you direct regular systematic focus beyond the near horizon of Box 1. Otherwise, lacking ready access to weak signals, your future will be starved of nonlinear ideas to develop. Regular meetings and deliverables make it more difficult to slide back into a habit of neglect.

The key point to take away here is that Hasbro has learned to see value in all three boxes, understands that they are interrelated, and has taken formal steps to ensure each gets the necessary attention.

Keeping It Simple: Basic Principles of the Three-Box Solution

Oliver Wendell Holmes is said to have observed, "I would not give a fig for the simplicity on this side of complexity, but I would give my life for the simplicity on the other side of complexity." The meaning of this quote is frequently debated, but I take it to mean that Holmes judged an idea or a tool by its ultimate effectiveness. Until it shows its mettle, he doesn't give a fig; he remains a skeptic. I use the quote to suggest that this book will show how this simple framework can prove its mettle by helping you tame the apparent complexities of leading innovation. The denser the tangle, the more useful the tool.

The deceptively simple Three-Box Solution has only a handful of principles:

- You should engage in both linear (Box 1) and nonlinear (Box 3) innovations to ensure leadership in the future.

- Success in Box 1 is the primary inhibitor of taking bold action in Box 3. You must develop the discipline of selectively forgetting the past (Box 2) or the past will prevent you from creating the future.

- Optimizing current business models in Box 1 and creating new business models in Box 3 must be pursued *simultaneously*, yet they call for different activities, skills, methods, metrics, mind-sets, and leadership approaches.

- Managing the three boxes is a journey, not a project. Businesses fail at it when they are sporadic rather than continuous in seeking balance. Like gardens that need regular watering and weeding, each box requires ongoing attention.

- Don't think about the future as a far-off time. The future is actually now because you are building it day by day.

The next five chapters draw on varied examples, including a coffee-roasting and beverage-brewing company, a global network of Protestant churches, and a large equipment-rental business. Each is distinctively accomplished in using one or more of the three boxes, and a couple of them are exceptional at keeping all three in balance. Most have faced powerful "forgetting" challenges. None of them would ever claim to have all the answers; indeed, the work of trying to sustain balance is automatically humbling.

We will look at the three boxes one by one in the next three chapters, moving from the future (Box 3) to the past (Box 2) and returning to the present (Box 1). The Three-Box Solution is a concept to communicate the balance of leadership for the here and now, forgetting the past, and creating the future as a three-ringed circus occurring simultaneously. We return to the theme of balance across the three boxes in chapters 5 and 6.

At the end of each chapter, you'll find *takeaways* that distill the core message in a way you can share with others in your organization. A *tools* section, also at the end of every chapter, includes discussion points, questionnaires, and activities to help you and your team apply the ideas and develop your own Three-Box Solution.

We begin with the future (Box 3) in chapter 2 because the future is about creation, and creation not only precedes everything else, but the task of creating the future really is where the problem of balance lies. You'll want to start with a cup of strong coffee.

Takeaways

- *Do not distract those who work in the core Box 1 business from their demanding performance goals.* Box 1 cannot execute Box 3 innovations. And that is OK. Remember that Box 3 cannot exist without Box 1. Also, what must be forgotten for the purposes of Box 3 may still be vitally important to Box 1.

- *Box 2 is the indispensable element of the Three-Box Solution.* Most organizations ignore Box 2 as they try to innovate their way to a new model. Even as old ideas and practices choke off the new future they're trying to create, organizations find it very difficult to overcome the power of the past. The more attention a company pays to Box 2, the more room there is for the Box 3 to achieve its goals. If Box 3 were an NFL quarterback, Box 2 would be the offensive line, providing time and flexibility in which to read the defense, execute, and, if necessary, improvise. Without a well-functioning Box 2 discipline, your Box 3 offense will be stagnant and predictable.

- *Good Box 3 hedging strategies are important.* In a regime of experimentation and learning, not every step along the way will be successful. You need to develop a process for hedging risk. That typically means testing assumptions through iterative learning stages that, over time, resolve uncertainty and either produce growing confidence or reveal the need for a reboot or exit. Hasbro's 1970s venture into Romper Room–branded nursery schools might have benefited from better testing and hedging.

- **Create formal processes that both serve the goals of Box 3 and increase the likelihood of achieving balance among all three boxes.** Sustainable Box 3 activities require both structure and accountability. Hasbro CEO Brian Goldner inaugurated "martini meetings" and the Future Now team to keep Hasbro moving forward on Box 3 ideas. The martini meetings served the further purpose of identifying situations in which the three boxes might intersect. This became procedural reinforcement of the boxes' relatedness and ultimately contributed to balance. On a personal time-management level, Goldner audits the amount of attention he devotes to each box every week.

- **Think of the Three-Box Solution as endlessly cyclical.** You are always preserving the present, destroying the past, and building the future. In other words, the business models, products, and services you create in Box 3 will at some point become your new Box 1.

- **The Three-Box Solution imposes on leaders a requirement for humility,** because it is essentially a strategy for taking action through continuous learning. Learning is intrinsically a humbling activity; to learn is to admit you don't know everything. Almost every aspect of the Three-Box Solution framework is intended to increase opportunities to listen and learn. In my experience, the most effective leaders also happen to be good listeners, are never arrogant, and are able to disregard rank and status in the service of finding the best ideas. The examples in later chapters will bear this out.

TOOLS

Tool 1: Assess Your Business

Crafting Three-Box Solutions will require you to look at the way your business operates through a new lens. The starting point is to understand the way things operate now. For instance:

- How easy or difficult is it for your business to generate, refine, incubate, and launch new business ideas?

- Has your company, business unit, or functional department developed ongoing processes for identifying emergent trends, based on weak signals, that are likely to affect your business in the coming years?

- Describe your current planning process. Does it incorporate the voices of maverick thinkers? Does your population of mavericks feel empowered or, conversely, stifled?

- Describe your current method for resource allocation. Does it earmark funds for high-risk projects?

- Describe your current performance management system. Does it support experiments with unknown outcomes?

- Describe your current approach to talent acquisition. In addition to keeping Box 1 well stocked, do you also recruit talent that would support tomorrow's business?

- What particular factors and conditions does your current success depend on? Which of these factors might change over time, thus putting current success at risk? Do you have formal processes to anticipate and prepare for these possible changes so as to cushion or even exploit their impact?

- How much time does your management team currently spend on Box 1 versus Boxes 2 and 3?

- What barriers prevent your management team from spending more time on Boxes 2 and 3?

Tool 2: Identify Weak Signals

After diagnosing your current situation, initiate conversations around Box 3 thinking. As a management team, identify the *weak signals* that potentially could transform your industry in the future. In particular, reflect on:

- ***Customer discontinuities***. Are today's biggest, fastest-growing, or most profitable customer segments likely to be the same ones in ten to fifteen years? Who will be your customers in the future? Are there small or emerging customer segments today that are using or even customizing your products or services in unconventional ways? Which nonconsumers today could potentially become consumers in the future? What would be their priorities?

- ***Technological discontinuities***. What disruptive technologies can open up new opportunity spaces?

- ***Nontraditional competitors***. Are today's most potent competitors likely to be the same ones in ten to fifteen years? Who will you be competing against in the future? And on what basis?

- ***New distribution channels***. Will there be fundamental changes in your go-to-market approach in the future? What possible supply-chain economies (or diseconomies) might your business face?

- ***Regulatory changes***. What are the potential regulatory reforms? What new opportunities might they open up for you?

2

Create the Future

Box 3 ideas for the nonlinear future are built from wisps of insight known as weak signals. In the case of the Keurig brewing system, the relevant insight was the rancid aroma of truly terrible office coffee, at a time when coffee was in the midst of an extraordinary renaissance.

John Sylvan, along with his former Colby College roommate Peter Dragone, conceived the idea for the Keurig coffee-brewing technology after Sylvan was inspired by a eureka moment. In the mid-1980s, before Starbucks had become a coast-to-coast sensation, Sylvan was working at a Boston-area high-tech company where his entry-level status required that he manage the office's coffee needs. He recognized a fundamental problem: the world of gourmet coffee had simply skipped over the workplace. Typical office coffee services provided large foil bags of mediocre grinds that were drip-brewed into glass or metal coffeepots, after which they sat on warming stations getting scorched and bitter. The first few cups might be sort of OK—coffee loses its freshness within twenty minutes of brewing—but eventually it fell to the John Sylvans of the world to discard the unappetizing last third or more of the old pot and make another.

"There's got to be a better way to do this" was Sylvan's reaction to the problem. Sylvan exemplifies a maverick sensibility that can be essential to Box 3 ideas of the kind that spring from the thought that *there has to be a better way.*

The cultivation of mavericks and their ideas is an important aspect of the Three-Box Solution. Maverick-driven transformations begin with an understanding that there is a problem. Most people stop at the problem statement; they see that a problem exists but just shake their heads and move on. However, mavericks, who are often more attuned to weak signals than are others, continue to turn the problem over in their heads until they conceptualize an unconventional solution and a market opportunity that the solution can exploit.

Sylvan and legions of other coffee drinkers had developed a taste for richer, darker coffee, thanks to chains like Starbucks and Peet's Coffee & Tea. Cup by cup, this education gradually expanded consumer tastes. Up to that point, office coffee services had more or less met expectations of what break-room coffee should taste like: a flavor known by such affectionate nicknames as "swill," "paint remover," and "battery acid." Most Americans had been trained from the 1950s on to view coffee in a utilitarian light: it was a caffeine-delivery system in which taste was a lower-order benefit.

With Starbucks, expectations changed in a big way. Flavor and freshness mattered as never before. In fact, the growing appreciation of flavor made freshness matter even more. Because of its high volume, Starbucks offered consumers a fresh brew in every cup. Those who stopped there on the way to work for a "tall" dark roast would then have to switch to the burnt remains of a pot brewed who knows when.

As Sylvan threw out the swill of one too many scorched pots and brewed another, he began to wonder why every cup of office coffee couldn't be fresh. Why wasn't there a high-quality coffee equivalent to the common tea bag? The quest led Sylvan to contact Dragone, and in 1992 the two of them founded Keurig.

Dick Sweeney joined them a year later, after they had filed for coffeemaker and "portion-pack" patents and were pitching for their first round of venture funding. Sweeney, about ten years older than his two cofounders, was brought on board because he had both manufacturing and product-development experience.

The weak signal for the Keurig leadership team wasn't simply the emergence of gourmet coffee shops. It was how the success of Starbucks and other coffee roasters had changed the context for coffee consumption *everywhere*—at home, in the office, in restaurants, on airplanes, in the service-department customer lounge at the car dealership. Wherever people got their best coffee of the day, they wanted a comparable experience everywhere else.

Together, Keurig's founders had growing confidence in their idea for fresh-brewed single servings of coffee. Said Sweeney, "The idea was that the only way to ensure a fresh cup of coffee is to brew it as you consume it—one cup at a time."

They had developed working prototypes for both the brewer and the portion packs, soon to be known as K-Cup packs. The one thing they lacked was a real understanding of coffee roasting and brewing. A perfect cup of coffee is like a perfect golf swing. There are a surprising number of variables: the quality of the beans and the roast, the fineness of the grind, the amount of coffee in the portion pack, the temperature and purity of the water, and the rate at which it passes through the grounds and filter. If one variable is out of kilter, the coffee suffers.

The Keurig team knew what it didn't know—a huge cognitive advantage for a fledgling organization charting its future. In late 1995, the team approached Green Mountain Coffee Roasters (GMCR), headquartered in Waterbury, Vermont, which was within scenic driving distance from Keurig's base in Boston and had a solid reputation as a quality roaster. Sweeney recalled, "I told them, 'We want an education in coffee—and a million dollars.'"

Eventually, Keurig got both, though the education part came first. Green Mountain tutored Keurig on the ins and outs of coffee sourcing and roasting and the variables that needed to align to produce a great cup of coffee. Kevin Sullivan, who arrived at Keurig in late 2003 and was appointed the company's chief technology officer, described that challenge by quoting one of GMCR's coffee experts:

> *I go to Sumatra twice a year. I pick the best bean. I roast it to within an inch of its life. I grind it to the perfect grind. It's going to make this fantastic cup of coffee! Then a consumer goes and scoops once or twice or thrice—or who knows how many times. Then they pour in who knows how much water, and everything I worked for is destroyed because they never get the amount of coffee right for the amount of water they pour. They just never do!*

Keurig's promise to Green Mountain and other coffee roasters was that it would remove human error from the portioning and brewing of a cup of coffee. Innovations in brewer engineering would make each cup as close as possible to perfection. And the brewer would deliver it with unprecedented speed, ease, and convenience.

Green Mountain made its initial investment in Keurig in 1996. In 2006, after increasing its stake in stages, GMCR owned 100 percent of Keurig. A dedicated team continued to work on Keurig as a Box 3 experiment. GMCR's revenues grew at a compounded rate of 65 percent per year during 2006–2014 and reached $4.7 billion by 2014. By then, Keurig accounted for roughly 25 percent of all coffeemakers sold in America. The company had sold over 45 million Keurig brewers and more than 30 billion K-Cup packs, or pods. By 2014, GMCR had become Keurig Green Mountain, with a market capitalization of $26 billion.

GMCR's Box 3 Leap

Before it began investing in Keurig, GMCR was well on its way to operating a highly successful Box 1 performance engine in the coffee-roasting and retailing industry. Now, with Keurig, it had a full-fledged Box 3 phenomenon on its books. But when Keurig first came knocking, GMCR might well have politely declined the meeting. It wasn't at all clear at the time what an innovation in brewing technology had to do with the coffee-roasting business. GMCR executives easily could have said, "Absolutely not! We are a coffee company, not a hardware company. We don't make coffee machines." To their credit, however, they saw a glimpse of the future in plastic cups shaped like tiny yogurt containers.

During the decade that passed between GMCR's initial investment and its acquisition of Keurig, the two organizations exerted a kind of gravitational pull on each other. GMCR helped Keurig understand the importance of quality roasting and consistent brewing. Keurig, which remained wary of becoming too much a captive of any single roaster, helped GMCR appreciate the unique potential of its business model, including that Keurig was committed to making deals with as many of the top roasters and coffee brands as it could. *Roaster neutrality* was the only way to satisfy consumers' quickly expanding tastes and loyalties, and it was the key to unlocking the full value of Keurig's business model.

But getting there was no cakewalk. As with any nonlinear innovation, there were numerous difficulties and setbacks. For example, in late 1993, the founders demonstrated an early brewer prototype in a meeting with Memorial Drive Trust, a potential venture-capital investor. But the machine leaked hot water on the conference room table and failed to produce a decent cup of coffee. Though the venture-capital firm liked the concept—and eventually became Keurig's main venture partner—on that day, it declined to fund it. As one of the firm's executives concluded, "These guys were not ready for prime time."[1]

The founders nonetheless persevered. They made progress on brewer performance, filed new patent applications, and forged early relationships with Dunkin' Donuts (which was interested in piloting the use of Keurig brewers in small, one-employee retail kiosks). On the strength of these developments, Keurig rekindled the interest of Memorial Drive Trust and soon secured its first venture funding.

Box 3 Hallmark Principles and Behaviors

Keurig was a 360-degree innovation that created a new product in a new way for an unmet customer need using a new business model. It had five core specifications:

- *A perfect cup of coffee every time.* Eliminate the variables, including elapsed time after brewing, that can ruin a fresh cup of coffee.

- *A premium coffee experience.* Implicit in the goal of perfect coffee every time was that Keurig would deliver premium products for which it would charge premium prices. By installing the brewer, Keurig would create a rich annuity of future revenues for the high-margin K-Cup pod—the "razor-and-blades" approach.[2]

- *A variety of coffees from which to choose.* Offer a wide range of roasts and flavors in line with expanding consumer tastes. That meant building relationships with multiple coffee roasters— again, the concept of roaster neutrality—rather than becoming the captive of only one.

- *Exceptional ease of use.* Design a brewer and portion packs that hide their internal complexity behind simple, enjoyable operation. Achieving that goal would require a high level of engineering expertise.

- *Outsource capital-intensive activities.* Own crucial technologies— brewer design, K-Cup pod design, and packaging line design— but outsource capital-intensive activities, such as manufacturing brewers and K-Cup pods, and product distribution. The success of this arrangement would require Keurig to design financial incentives for its ecosystem partners so that the arrangement would be a "win-win."

The future that you work toward every day is a sometimes fragile venture. There are numerous points where the business you are building must face unforeseen risks and threats. That's to be expected. Box 3 ventures are filled with uncertainty and powered by experimentation. You should embrace risks as learning opportunities and see variance as a window into possible new directions and unforeseen benefits.

A Box 1 business by comparison is quite stable, conducted in a familiar, well-understood environment in which you can measure performance precisely and where you should control risk and see variance as a sign of trouble. You must judge progress in Box 3 by different criteria than you would apply in Box 1 (see table 2-1).

TABLE 2-1

Managing the present versus creating the future

Objectives	Box 1 Manage performance	Box 3 Create opportunities
Inputs	Unambiguous, objective data regarding linear changes affecting:	Weak signals regarding nonlinear changes affecting:
	• Current customers	• Nonconsumers
	• Current competitors	• Nontraditional competitors
	• Known technologies	• New or emerging technologies
Strategic emphasis	Linear innovations that contribute to:	Nonlinear innovations that require:
	• Making the numbers	• Testing assumptions
	• Enhancing current competencies	• Building new competencies
	• Reducing risk	• Embracing risk taking
	• Eliminating ambiguity and deviation	• Experimentation, learning, adaptation
	• Variance reduction	• Variance expansion
	• Efficiency	• Flexibility

To emphasize the differences between Box 1 and Box 3—and to literally remind people of when they need to pass from Box 1 to Box 3 thinking—the CEO of Assurant Solutions, Craig Lemasters, explained how the company put a sign at the entrance to the building: "We started a Box 3 initiative called Assurant Solutions Digital. We placed an image of BOX THREE in the entrance to the building of Assurant Solutions Digital to emphasize that the Box 3 dedicated team must act and behave differently and use different discipline as compared to the Box 1 performance engine." (See the photos from Assurant Solutions on the following page.)

In Box 3, you must regularly make important decisions based on incomplete information, sometimes without fully appreciating the extent of their implications and risks. This was the environment in which Keurig operated—constantly adapting to new information and

Source: Assurant Solutions. Used with permission.

conditions. (Dick Sweeney later joked that "there were times when I thought I might be one cup of coffee away from living in a Maytag box under the Harvard Bridge.")

What accounted for Keurig's success? A great idea was only the beginning. Great execution was an indispensable factor as well. The need to execute Box 3 strategies at a very high level explains why even the simplest frameworks are so difficult to apply successfully in the real world. Keurig's leaders executed every aspect of their strategy with determination, ingenuity, and discipline. Also decisively important was their reliance on a handful of general principles that I see used again and again by successful innovators as hallmarks of stellar Box 3 efforts:

- They placed smaller bets first before placing bigger bets.

- They exercised courageous, adaptive leadership.

- They built new Box 3 capabilities and processes as needed.

- They tested critical assumptions.

- They developed a Box 3 culture.

For the balance of this chapter, we will look more closely at how these interlocking ingredients combined to enable a Box 3 breakthrough.

Placing the Smaller Bet First

A fundamental element of the Three-Box Solution is placing smaller bets before placing bigger bets as an effective way to reduce the risk of Box 3 ideas.

From its inception, Keurig saw two desirable markets: the commercial or office ("away from home") market and the consumer ("at home") market. The household market was vast compared to the office market—the Atlantic Ocean to Lake Erie. For Keurig, however, it was not an either/or proposition. It wanted to participate in both markets, but it chose to pursue them in separate stages. This allowed the company to leverage what it learned from the office market (1998) to make the most of its later launch into the household market (2004).

Building the brand and distribution. Trying to crack both markets at once would have taxed company resources to the breaking point. Even worse, it would have denied Keurig the opportunity to build brand awareness, reputation, and loyalty among office coffee drinkers. Focusing first on the office market would allow the company to collect a few years' worth of valuable feedback on what customers did and didn't like about the Keurig system in the office; almost all of that feedback would translate well to the home market. Over the years, soliciting and acting on customer feedback became a Keurig addiction as potent as caffeine.

Perfecting the brewer technology. Another benefit of the smaller niche bet was that there were thorny technical issues to work through before the company could successfully exploit the at-home market. First and foremost, a big price-performance chasm needed to be bridged. Keurig's office brewers were extremely expensive—selling for as much as $1,000 per unit—and Keurig would require both engineering breakthroughs and improved manufacturing efficiencies to produce high-quality, reasonably priced household versions. The bifurcated marketing strategy would give Keurig time to morph its office models into lean kitchen-counter appliances that reliably delivered great coffee at a price home users would be willing to pay.

That promised to be a lot of work. Just getting early versions of the office brewers to perform reliably proved to be challenging enough. According to Sweeney, in proof-of-concept trials, Keurig distributed brewers to about twenty-five Boston-area businesses. The firms were invited to try out the system and provide feedback. It was like the out-of-town opening of a Broadway show—an opportunity to work out the kinks.

And there were definitely kinks. The brewers often broke down and had to be either repaired or replaced. Keurig had to keep in reserve as many replacement units as they had brewers in the field. Even so, said Sweeney, "We didn't have people calling and yelling, 'Get this freaking thing out of here!' Instead, what they said was, 'We love this. Get it to work!' So that encouraged additional investment. It was a low-cost experiment that validated our hunch that we were on the right track." Indeed, low-cost learning is precisely the point of smaller bets.

Validating the system's economics. Another aspect of the learning curve involved whether the economics of the office market would prove to be tolerant of expensive coffee technology. If Keurig could successfully establish its premium positioning in the office, that would likely bode well for the at-home market.

In addition to the high cost of Keurig's office brewers, the K-Cup pod would sell for roughly $.50 apiece—five times what it cost to produce a single cup from a traditional coffeemaker. Many offices provided free coffee to employees as a perk (no pun intended), and Keurig's sales force got some early positive indicators from office managers. Many were especially enthusiastic about the Keurig system, partly because the Keurig brewer was convenient, mess-free, and would modestly enhance staff productivity; no low-ranking employee would need to be delegated, like John Sylvan, to periodically brew another pot of coffee. But office managers also liked something else. A senior executive described the delight of some office managers when the new brewing system launched: "Usually, it's difficult for office managers to please anyone. *The copier's broken . . . We're out of paper clips . . . The computer network's down . . .* This was a chance for the office manager to be a hero."[3] So a $.50 K-Cup pod may have been pricey, but the employees were actually happy. Complaints about bad coffee disappeared overnight.

There was also a compelling upside for coffee service vendors: where they might have earned only $.02 per cup from a traditionally brewed pot, they could earn $.10 a cup from the Keurig system. This helped turn them into enthusiastic promoters of the Keurig brand to their customers who hadn't yet tried it.

Developing the K-Cup pod manufacturing technology. Serving only the office market also gave Keurig time to work through the design and fabrication of the automated packaging machinery needed to manufacture the K-Cup pods. During the office-brewer trials, Sweeney remembers joining other Keurig employees in a back room, manually assembling K-Cup pods in a frenzy to supply enough of them to keep the trials going—clearly, not a permanent solution.

When the system launched in 1998, Keurig had orders from office coffee services for fifteen thousand brewers. It estimated it needed to be able to assemble and distribute enough K-Cup pods to meet potential demand of forty cups per day per brewer—a daily output of as many as six hundred thousand single portions. Keurig's immediate future was therefore riding on those packaging lines. The company had signed up its first few affiliate coffee roasters, including GMCR, to provide an assortment of coffees in K-Cup pods. The packaging lines were to be located at the roasters' facilities, so it was crucial the machinery be delivered on time to ensure the fifteen thousand brewers would actually have something to brew.

However, the supplier hired to fabricate the packaging lines refused to release the first unit, destined for GMCR, unless Keurig agreed to pay extra (well above the supplier's bid) for the time and trouble of accommodating several changes Keurig had made to the specs. Nick Lazaris, Keurig's CEO at that time, was blindsided by the demand. It felt like a hostage situation, with the packaging line—and Keurig's ability to provision its customers—used as leverage to wring more money out of the job. Any further delay would damage Keurig's new relationships with customers and partners. Lazaris believed he had no choice but to negotiate a quick solution with the vendor. Although Keurig's lead venture investor was infuriated and wanted to unleash the lawyers, Lazaris insisted that standing on principle would take too long to reach an uncertain outcome and the packaging line was already overdue at GMCR. Ultimately, the Keurig team members swallowed their anger and cut a deal, but Lazaris had Sweeney look for alternate suppliers of future packaging lines.

With the successful launch of its office product line, Keurig had revenues of $22 million by 2002. It had been profitable since 2000 and was the leading single-serve player in the office market. This start was, to be sure, very good, but it was only a small fraction of what the company was about to become. In short, it was the small bet that paved the way to betting big on the consumer market.

In a May 2003 letter to GMCR stakeholders, reporting on the progress of the company's investment in Keurig, GMCR CEO Bob Stiller wrote, in what turned out to be dramatic understatement, "I believe Keurig and its roaster partners will successfully develop the 'at home market' and, as a result, the value of Green Mountain's investment in Keurig will increase over the next 3–5 years."[4]

Exercising Adaptive Leadership

The decision Lazaris made to negotiate with the packaging line supplier is a good example of showing both courageous leadership and context-aware adaptability, given Keurig's most urgent priority *at that moment.*

Strong leadership often comes down to having a sure grasp of what is most important in context and keeping the business focused on it. At the time, nothing mattered more to Keurig than acquiring the packaging technology it needed to provide K-Cup pods to its new customers. Failing that could have meant failing as a business. Under other circumstances—in a Box 1 business, for example—enforcing the terms of a binding contract would have been more important than placating a balky supplier. But Box 3 is by definition more tolerant of risks undertaken for an important cause.

In a broader sense, Keurig was led by a group of exceptionally determined executives. John Whoriskey, who joined Keurig in 2002 to help launch its consumer business, described a resilient, even scrappy, company culture: "A lot of our success was really just driven by the fact that we weren't going to fail—that we were going to be successful and we were going to will our way to success across the board." What follows are some of the areas in which courageous, adaptive leadership led to success.

Cultivating the ecosystem. Ultimately, the contentious experience with its packaging line supplier served as a useful lesson to Keurig about controlling its own destiny. Sweeney put the experience to use both in the near term (by looking for new packaging line suppliers) and in the long term (by cultivating relationships with a number of contract manufacturers in Asia capable of cost-efficiently manufacturing brewers for the at-home market). Once it entered the at-home market, Keurig's brewer and portion-pack output would grow respectively from 800,000 and 600 million in 2008 to 8 million and 6 billion in 2012. "We grew at an exponential rate," said Sweeney. "We couldn't have scaled up our business that fast without the network of contract manufacturers." Creating the future successfully thus required envisioning not only the current ecosystem in which Keurig must compete effectively but also the one to which it would potentially have to scale.

That made it especially important for Keurig to develop and maintain strong, incentive-based relationships with all of its partners. From affiliate roasters to contract manufacturers, the company learned the value of stressing that all parties ultimately profit from long-lasting relationships. Beginning in 2010, Sweeney began convening annual summits for Keurig's manufacturing partners. At first, the attendees were nervous to see so many of their competitors in the room, especially when the agenda turned to sensitive pricing issues. But they got over it. "The way we set it up, I said, 'Look, to the outside world you're competitors. In Keurig's world you're all family, so get to know your cousins. We're going to need each other.' It's worked well."

Validating the premium position. As Keurig transitioned from serving the niche office-coffee-service market to going all in on the consumer mass market, it faced the question of whether, and by how much, to compromise its identity as a premium brand. Businesses moving between niche and mass markets often must answer this question. When Toyota went in the opposite direction—from mass market to luxury niche—it chose to create the new Lexus brand to rid itself of the corporate brand's down-market baggage.

In Keurig's case, however, the "baggage" of its office market experience was more an asset than a liability. Long before its at-home product launched, office consumers of Keurig coffee frequently would ask whether a home version of the system was in the works. It made sense not to mess with the premium experience. But complicating the decision were the actions of some of Keurig's heavyweight competitors. Swiss company Nestlé had launched a single-serving espresso maker, Nespresso, in Europe in 1986, introducing its household version to the US market five years later.[5] Nespresso machines brew espresso from pods made by Nestlé. However, espresso was far less popular than the coffee most Americans drank; they preferred to sip hot java from big cups.[6] Among US companies, Procter & Gamble (P&G) had launched Mr. Coffee Home Café, manufactured by Black & Decker (it brewed mainly P&G's Folgers coffee brands), and Sara Lee launched Senseo, manufactured by Philips (it brewed Douwe Egberts coffee brands). These two competitors were planning to pursue a low-end strategy, with brewers priced one-third below the cost of Keurig's models and portion packs at less than half.

News of competitors' intended strategy caused enough nervousness at Keurig that there was some second-guessing about sticking with the premium positioning. But it had been core to the company's strategy, identity, and success to date, and leadership remained committed to delivering a premium experience that included benefits, such as a wide selection of coffees from multiple roasters, that others would be unable to match. Nonetheless, these were all assumptions that needed to be tested. (See the next section on the importance of testing critical assumptions.)

Deciding what not to do and be. In its early days, Keurig considered producing its own branded line of coffees. Perhaps the wisest decision Keurig's leaders made at the time was to abandon that plan. Had they not made a clean break with that idea, they would have become rivals rather than partners of roasters, undercutting the potency of their business model.

The leadership agenda in Box 3 is to continually evaluate the relevance of even core ideas and identities. For example, Keurig eventually stopped seeing itself as exclusively a brewer of coffees. It added teas and other hot beverages (cider, hot chocolate, some soups). It announced plans to debut a new Box 3 venture, a cold-beverage system dubbed Keurig Kold, in late 2015. For that venture, Keurig sealed deals with Coca-Cola and Dr. Pepper Snapple Group.

Showing courage by killing a sunk investment. It is easy to become irrationally committed to investments you've already made, even bad ones. Yet it takes a lot of leadership courage to acknowledge that an investment has been misspent.

Keurig faced such a situation not long before launching its at-home business. The management team realized that the brewer intended for the consumer market, which Keurig had hired outside parties to help develop, suffered from serious cost and performance problems.

Not only was the design of the brewer, known as the B100, fundamentally flawed (in part because of a thirty-minute wait for water to heat), but it also cost more than twice as much to produce as most customers were likely to be willing to pay. If this was the brewer Keurig hoped to ride into the at-home market, the management team members agreed that it wasn't up to the job.

They made a bold decision in late 2002. They would immediately begin development of a new home brewer, to be named the B50, to replace the yet-to-launch B100. This bold decision proved pivotal to Keurig's successful entry into the at-home market.

Building New Box 3 Capabilities and Processes

In 2003, there were only ten people in the Keurig engineering group. It's not surprising, then, that the company sometimes embraced outsourcing as the most expedient solution. But for Keurig to become a business able to parlay its Box 3 roots into an engine of successive breakthroughs, it would need an abundance of skills different from those typically found in "a countertop appliance company."

Embedding high-tech engineering capabilities. Kevin Sullivan, whose background included stints in GE's jet engine and aerospace divisions, would reshape the engineering mission at Keurig more along the lines of developing advanced technology than of building traditional appliances. "When I saw what went on inside the brewer," he commented, "it was clear to me this device is nothing like any other kitchen appliance. Rather than [contract out to] people who had experience in mixers and toasters and simple kitchen appliances, we needed high-tech people to solve the internal problems. And we needed to own that technology." The ramifications of this shift, which changed the way the company thought about talent and mission, are still paying dividends at Keurig.

Sullivan continued, "Our software people came from companies like Raytheon, where they program missiles. Our hardware people, who developed the brewers' water tanks, had designed heating and industrial controls in previous jobs."

By 2014, there were more than four hundred people in Sullivan's group.

Fostering systems thinking. The difference in the size of the engineering group between 2003 and 2014 is more than just numerical. Sullivan's background at GE taught him to value a systems-based engineering approach. Systems engineering means understanding not only your own piece of the engineered product, but also how it fits with the other pieces and contributes to the product's overall objectives.

Consequently, in building up Keurig's capability, Sullivan looked for people who were both "deep and broad"—deep experts within their own design areas, but also with a breadth of knowledge about the design of elements adjacent to their areas of expertise—in other words, great designers of trees who also understood the context of the forest. "That's what makes us a success," Sullivan said.

Sullivan described how he himself became both deep and broad as a young GE mechanical engineer: "I started in aircraft engines. I went into weapon systems. I did refrigerators and satellites. But along the way, in typical GE fashion, I had to learn about electronics. I had to learn about software. I had to learn about a whole bunch of things that had nothing to do with mechanical [engineering] on my GE journey to be a general manager in a leadership position in a technology category. All of the folks I've hired are the same."

This idea is important. Versatility is an enabling Box 3 value. Creative individuals who can see the greater picture find many more sources of inspiration than those who focus narrowly on their own circumscribed domains. To enhance that exposure, Sullivan encouraged engineers not only to understand adjacent disciplines but also to actively cross-train in them. For example, experts in coffee blends were also versed in every aspect of brewer technology and operation.

It is almost impossible to predict the potential benefits of purposefully building a team that possesses both depth and breadth—only that these benefits will be numerous. Conversely, it is rather easy to predict that a narrowly focused team will produce nothing surprising. That's not always a bad thing. As you will see in chapter 4, Box 1, where variance is unwelcome, actually benefits from a disciplined, well-executed focus on narrow and known domains. In Box 1, there is value in sticking to your knitting. In Box 3, you throw out the pattern.

Another aspect of Sullivan's talent acquisition strategy is that it attracts people who are both curious and eager to discover new ways of doing things. If you allow such people to pay attention to what their colleagues are up to, their curiosity and eagerness to learn are more likely to be stimulated. You end up with people who like nothing more than to troubleshoot a challenging problem.

In the movie *Apollo 13*, the scenes in which a small team of engineers in Houston tries to improvise a way of purifying the air on the crippled spacecraft are filled with creative energy. Though the engineers are under extraordinary pressure, you can feel that they are also both exhilarated and confident in their ability to find solutions. That same kind of confidence is what Sullivan was working to create at Keurig by allowing a new capability to flourish.

The leadership team used the shortcomings of the outsourced brewer as (1) a teachable moment about the importance of wholly owning the core technologies and (2) a rallying point for sharpening Keurig's in-house engineering capabilities. In the near term, this approach led to a far more promising home-market brewer entry. Even better, in the long term, it left Keurig with a substantially expanded— more versatile and more energized—engineering capability.

The Three-Box Solution often requires an ability to think and act simultaneously in multiple time frames. Just as Sweeney envisioned both current and future manufacturing needs, Sullivan's recognition that a revamped engineering group would deliver both immediate and long-term benefits likewise exemplifies balanced multidimensional decision making.

Controlling the packaging technology. Keurig designed the packaging lines and continued over time to modify them to improve their performance and output. Retaining proprietary control over design of the packaging technology yielded several benefits. For one thing, because the lines were located on each roaster's premises and because the packaging technique removed the oxygen from the K-Cup pods, each roaster's coffees were packaged fresh and stayed fresh in the pods for a very long time. Further, improvements over the years to the packaging lines increased output from a hundred to twelve hundred K-Cup pods per minute. If Keurig hadn't owned the technology for this vital equipment, boosting performance to such an extent would have been extremely difficult.

Another beneficial aspect of the packaging line operation arose from a key decision Keurig made early on about something *not* to do. It could have chosen to have roasters ship their coffees to a Keurig facility for packaging in K-Cup pods and, from there, distribution to retail channels. But having designed its business model to emphasize roaster neutrality, it instead maximized the model's efficiency by having the affiliate roasters package and ship their own branded K-Cup pods. This eliminated steps in the process that would have added both time and cost across the board—and for no good purpose.

Consequently, besides ensuring the availability to Keurig users of a variety of coffees, roaster neutrality allowed the supply chain to be operated more efficiently and accountably. Of course, Keurig shouldered the added complexity of inventing and continuing to improve the design of the packaging lines, but it offloaded to roasters the responsibility for manufacturing the K-Cup pods and filling the supply chain with enough volume to meet growing demand. Keurig, in turn, benefited from the roasters' established reputations and from their marketing efforts on behalf of their own branded K-Cup pods.

And, of course, *all* parties made money on every K-Cup pod sold. Forging mutually profitable relationships with roasters was at the heart of the business model. Outsourcing K-Cup pod manufacture was simply a rational way to make the business model more efficient.

Testing Critical Assumptions

Only dumb luck can save a Box 3 project from missteps caused by untested faulty assumptions. If a failure is in your future, you want it to come fast; testing assumptions is the best way to reveal an ill-conceived project. From the beginning, Keurig made an enthusiastic discipline of gathering and analyzing evidence to test critical assumptions, learn, and adapt.

Testing premium positioning. Keurig recognized at an early point that entering the at-home market might put its premium position at risk. Consequently, it undertook a variety of research initiatives to test home consumers' receptivity to a premium experience and the price points necessary to deliver it. By the time it was ready to make its move, the company had developed reasonably high confidence that the premium strategy was solid and that the at-home market would break in its direction. Research suggested home consumers would be receptive to brewers priced between $129 and $199 and the K-Cup pod at $.50 apiece (see the sidebar, "Testing the Home-Brew Waters").

The math of Keurig's premium economics proved to be highly favorable—profitable to itself and pleasing to consumers. The *New York Times* published an article that attempted to get a handle on portion-pack economics.[10] It calculated that the per-pound price of coffee dispensed one K-Cup pod at a time ranged from over two to more than four times higher than consumers would pay to buy a pound of beans, grind it at home, and brew it themselves. It's easy, therefore, to see how much potential profit lives inside a single nine- to fifteen-gram portion pack.

The *Times* also looked at the question of how great a premium different consumers placed on convenience and ease: "Where single-serve

Testing the Home-Brew Waters

During the years between the launch of its office (1998) and consumer (2004) product lines, Keurig stayed busy doing homework on what it called the "at-home" market. From 1999 through 2001, it conducted a variety of customer surveys, focus groups, and home field tests aimed at gauging coffee drinkers' interest in, and expectations of, a home version of the Keurig system, along with their tolerance of particular price points for both brewers and portion packs.

The conventional wisdom for entrants bent on capturing mass-market customers for single-serving coffee in the home was that they would need to aim for the low end. Given Keurig's founding mission to deliver a premium product and experience, it needed to test that low-end assumption. Naturally, Keurig had assumptions of its own, including that Starbucks and others had trained a large segment of coffee drinkers to expect high quality, freshness, flavor, and variety. The ability to meet those expectations would justify a premium price. Here is some of what the company learned:[7]

Keurig conducted intercept interviews in 2000 with customers entering or leaving relevant retail settings, such as Starbucks or Dunkin' Donuts. It screened respondents on the basis of their regular consumption of gourmet coffee, both at home and away (including some who were familiar with Keurig or other single-serve offerings in the workplace).

- Respondents consumed an average of two to three cups of gourmet coffee daily, both at home and away.

- Eighty-eight percent expressed interest in the Keurig system. People were intrigued by the convenience, ease of use, and lack of mess associated with brewing in portion packs.

coffee falls on that spectrum depends on whether you regard coffee as something you make or something you drink." Keurig's business model had bet on the army of drinkers, not the relatively fewer makers. For most coffee drinkers, convenience, speed, flavor, and freshness were values worth paying for.

- Upward of 75 percent expressed interest in buying a Keurig brewer based solely on a verbal explanation. After a demonstration of the system, purchase interest increased to more than 90 percent.

- Forty-four percent of those who had coffee from a system demonstration said they would be willing to pay $.50 for a K-Cup pod. Those who consumed more coffee daily were willing to pay a premium for both the brewer and the K-Cup pod.

Keurig conducted at-home trials in which a focus group of consumers received a commercial brewer to try out at home.

- In interviews, testers (who were required to buy K-Cup pods at $.50 apiece during the trial) "consistently referenced great-tasting coffee with a system that was fast and convenient."[8] They also valued cup-to-cup consistency of flavor, the variety of coffee selections, and the ease of prep and lack of mess.

- Participants in the trial reported that their coffee consumption at home increased (to 2.25 cups a day), while their consumption away from home went down.

- Participants identified an acceptable brewer price range between $129 and $199. They considered a price higher than $200 "to be a luxury purchase for which more consideration would be required."[9] And they paid the $.50 price per K-Cup pod without blinking.

Together, these results, when combined with earlier and externally sourced market research and Keurig-commissioned internet surveys, demonstrated a relatively high tolerance for Keurig's premium position in the at-home market.

Building a better brewer. What needed more testing, however, were the design specifications and manufacturing costs of the planned home version of Keurig's brewer technology. It was one thing to scrap the outsourced B100 brewer and start from scratch to build a worthy alternative. Less clear was how to solve the various technical and cost problems.

This was a frightening time in the company's history. When Sweeney contemplated living in a Maytag box under the Harvard Bridge, it was because Keurig was within six months of exhausting its capital. The consumer market was a make-or-break play. Keurig could not possibly launch with an inferior brewer. The replacement had to be a winner.

The team didn't go into the effort cold. It already had some insights on how to improve on the B100. Keurig hadn't launched the B100 brewer into retail channels but had sold modest numbers on its web-site. Feedback on the B100 alerted Keurig to, among other things, the unacceptability of the half-hour wait for its eight-cup water tank to heat up to the ideal brewing temperature. That pointed it toward the need to make smarter trade-offs in the new B50 between the ability to brew a number of successive cups and the ability to brew each cup at the ideal temperature.

The solutions would depend on how home users would actually use the brewer. Office models might, on average, brew upward of forty cups a day. Based on field tests, the team determined that home users would probably brew no more than four or five cups a day. The team therefore decided to shrink the size of the B50 water tank, which appreciably reduced the cost of the brewer. One critical question remained: how long is too long to wait for water to heat before brew-ing? The likely answer was "not very long"; much more than a minute would test most users' patience.

In a succession of working prototypes, the team shrank the water tank to three cups and at the same time used software, low-cost sen-sors, and microprocessor technology to accelerate and regulate the heating process. In response to customer pleas for larger cups of coffee, brewer versions were developed to allow for cups sized between four and ten ounces.

Users also gave feedback on styling, never much of an issue for office brewers but significant now that the brewer was on consumers' kitchen counters. The B100 had too big a footprint. The B50 would be lean by comparison.

Lowering brewer cost. The fact that a smaller brewer could both be simpler and require less material would be helpful in controlling cost. And the B50's use of low-cost sensor and microprocessor technology would likewise contribute to making it both economical and more efficient. But adding advanced technology and making the brewer smaller would not be enough. The B100 had been manufactured in Alabama and cost roughly $250 to produce. Keurig believed the ideal price point was around $150. John Whoriskey was willing to break even at that price. The razor-and-blades business model made breaking even sustainable. But the brewer would have to be manufactured in China. Sweeney's work to establish relationships with offshore manufacturers helped make the home market feasible while maintaining Keurig's premium position.

Improving the K-Cup pod. Through trial-and-error experimentation, Keurig kept modifying the K-Cup pod innards to accommodate ever-larger payloads of ground coffee beans, a multiyear journey that eventually won Keurig partnerships with Starbucks, Peet's, Caribou, and other roasters of richer, stronger coffees (see the sidebar, "The Evolving K-Cup Pod"). By 2015, Keurig offered nearly four hundred varieties of K-Cup pods representing sixty different brands.

Slipstreaming on rivals' marketing budgets. One of the underrated benefits of validating your assumptions is that it gives you the confidence to do—or not do—other things. As the B50 neared completion,

The Evolving K-Cup Pod

In essence, a K-Cup pod is both the package and the product: a plastic container with a sealed foil lid. Inside the container is a filter that holds a single serving of ground coffee. Before brewing, each K-Cup pod enclosed in the cradle of a brewer is pierced top and bottom so that heated water can flow through it (see figure 2-1). That means the filter must be carefully suspended within the K-Cup pod so it remains out of reach of the sharp discharge nozzle that pierces the bottom of the container and would otherwise damage it.

FIGURE 2-1

How the K-Cup pod works

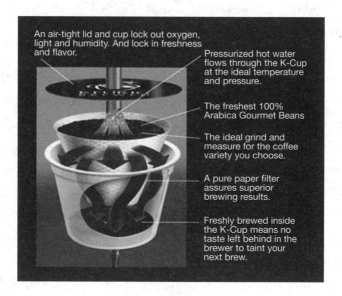

An air-tight lid and cup lock out oxygen, light and humidity. And lock in freshness and flavor.

Pressurized hot water flows through the K-Cup at the ideal temperature and pressure.

The freshest 100% Arabica Gourmet Beans

The ideal grind and measure for the coffee variety you choose.

A pure paper filter assures superior brewing results.

Freshly brewed inside the K-Cup means no taste left behind in the brewer to taint your next brew.

Source: Diagram copyright Keurig. Used with permission.

Keurig was able to feel secure that it would offer quality performance at a price home consumers were willing to pay. And it would live up to the reputation it had earned in the office market.

Major competitors entered the single-serve coffee market for at-home consumers. Besides P&G and Sara Lee, Kraft launched Tassimo,

The progressive refinement of the K-Cup pod occurred over several years as Keurig persistently tried to win over roasters of stronger, richer coffees. The technical limit on coffee strength was the amount of ground coffee each K-Cup pod could hold. The original version held roughly nine grams. That was enough, said Kevin Sullivan, "to make a light cup of coffee that was typical of the New England taste profile." But it was not nearly enough to produce a cup of coffee that would impress a taster at Starbucks.

In visits to Starbucks and other West Coast roasters over the years, Keurig executives grew tired of the slow headshake of rejection. But it was motivating. In terms of making changes, said Sullivan, "The difficulty with the system is that, once you have brewers out there, you are locked into a geometry and you can't make [the portion pack] bigger. You can only work on the inside." Since the filter in the initial K-Cup pod version was conical, that shape became the focus of attention.

The first K-Cup pod improvement featured a fluted filter with a less-severe conical shape that was also truncated at the bottom to keep it clear of the discharge nozzle. This version was able to hold twelve grams of coffee. Starbucks noted the improvement but said it was still not enough.

"Every year we'd go back and say, 'How about this?'" said Sullivan. Then would come the headshake. Eventually, Keurig produced a longer version of the fluted filter, capable of holding fourteen grams of coffee. "Then Starbucks told us, 'Gee, you're really getting there. That is our taste profile.'" That opened the door to discussions that eventually led to a Starbucks line of K-Cup pods.

manufactured by Braun (and mainly brewing Kraft's Maxwell House coffee brands). In the run-up to the 2004 holiday shopping season, competitors planned expensive advertising campaigns just to build market awareness of the benefits of single-serve brewing at home. Whoriskey made the decision not to spend on media advertising. Keurig would benefit from its competitors' large marketing budgets, which would build awareness of the category and attract shoppers to retail outlets. And when the shoppers arrived at the biggest department store chains and at gourmet outlets, such as Williams-Sonoma, Keurig was on hand to conduct live demonstrations, urging consumers to "spoil" themselves with its at-home coffeehouse experience. Keurig's research revealed that the likelihood of purchase increased dramatically when consumers saw the system in action and tasted the coffee.

When the dust cleared after the 2004 holiday shopping season, Keurig had outsold all of its competitors combined.

Creating a Box 3 Culture

By the time Whoriskey and Sullivan joined Keurig, a number of Box 3 behaviors had begun to take root within the company. Certainly it was self-evident that Keurig was born from a nonlinear insight, one that completely discarded established ideas about how to brew coffee. And the razor-and-blades business model, powered by roaster-neutral partnerships, was presciently designed to produce success.

What was missing, however, were the skills, structures, and attitudes that could make nonlinear Box 3 thinking sustainable and repeatable—in short, a habit. That was where Keurig leaders focused their attention. Here are some of the values they fostered:

- *Restlessness and dissatisfaction.* Complacency is the enemy of Box 3 thinking. Great breakthrough innovations are never finished. A Box 3 culture strives to surpass its own past successes. By 2015, Keurig Green Mountain was ready to enter the cold-beverage market.

- *Openness to outside ideas and skills.* Like the air that circulates on airplanes, a closed system can become stale. Fresh air requires a conscious commitment to bring new capabilities and outside perspectives into an established company. Such practices as

Sweeney's annual supplier summits and Sullivan's habit of looking far afield for unconventional talent help add new voices.

- *Eagerness for challenges.* The best engineers and designers enjoy
  testing themselves under pressure. Sullivan tells a story about
  his team fixing a brewer problem overnight. The fact that
  the problem was brought to their attention by Keurig Green
  Mountain CEO Brian Kelley added both to the challenge and
  to the pressure. Kelley had given brewers to each of his brothers, and they all complained about a grating noise the water
  pump made. The engineers had grown used to the noise, but
  they tinkered with the pump, adding bumpers and changing
  some materials until the pump produced a pleasing instead of
  grating sound. Kelley was astonished that the team arrived at a
  successful fix by the following day. "We've built up these muscles
  of innovation and capability, teamwork, and camaraderie,"
  said Sullivan—to the point where fixing a noisy water pump is
  recreational.

- *Experimentation and adaptation.* Experiments are the best way
  to test hypotheses. You learn from the results, make necessary
  changes, experiment again, and learn more. As the body of
  learning grows, small bets give way to larger bets made with
  greater confidence. In some respects, Sullivan's long-term
  project to build up the muscles of innovation was itself a long
  series of experiments, each formed by new needs and new
  information.

- *Uncommon sense.* When you're competing with the likes of P&G
  and Kraft, it's only common sense to anticipate you'll need to
  spend millions on an advertising campaign. But a strong Box
  3 culture can show a preference, when needed, for uncommon

sense—hence, Whoriskey's decision to invest Keurig's marketing budget in less conventional ways during the 2004 holiday shopping season.

- *Plan B flexibility.* Finally, because Box 3 cultures typically must tolerate conditions of high uncertainty and risk, they need to adapt quickly to changing circumstances. Keurig's early vulnerability to its packaging line supplier underscored the importance of having plan B options. Over time, Keurig became a good improviser, ensuring operational flexibility for itself.

For me, these values call to mind a vivid metaphor from Elizabeth Gilbert's excellent memoir *Eat, Pray, Love.* In it, she describes one of life's fundamental balancing acts: "We gallop through our lives like circus performers balancing on two speeding side-by-side horses— one foot is on the horse called 'fate,' the other is on the horse called 'free will.' And the question you have to ask every day is—which horse is which? Which horse do I need to stop worrying about because it's not under my control, and which do I need to steer with concentrated effort?"[11]

Though Gilbert is writing about personal conduct, her metaphor applies equally well to organizations and their leaders. Across every activity, a business must continually ask itself, Which horse is which? *The horse of free will can be steered, but the horse of fate cannot be controlled.* Successful people and organizations know how to keep their focus on what they can control. As a result, they waste very little time and energy on the uncontrollable horse.

Gilbert isn't suggesting that you should ignore the horse you can't control. On the contrary, you need to understand, respect, and work to hedge against the destructive potential of uncontrollable fates. Because Box 3 in particular requires a high tolerance of risk and uncertainty, you will need to be especially mindful of that rogue horse's potential mischief. Thus, the main "controllable" levers for hedging against unwelcome circumstances are experimentation, learning, and adaptation—profiting from new information and rising certainty, thereby reducing risk and enabling bigger bets.

Finally, Box 3 success depends on your ability to apply the concept of planned opportunism. As I described it in chapter 1, planned opportunism is the discipline of becoming as well prepared as possible to act on whatever circumstances fate either bestows or inflicts upon you. From Sullivan's campaign to bolster his engineering group to Sweeney's creation of strong partner relations and Whoriskey's research initiatives in advance of the consumer launch, Keurig was well prepared to exercise planned opportunism in Box 3. These are all instances of exerting control over what you can in order to improve the odds that fate, which you cannot control, will more likely operate in your favor.

The Challenge of Sustaining Balance across All Three Boxes

Since many of its main K-Cup pod patents expired in late 2012, Keurig faced an influx of new competition to which it responded in a number of ways. Anticipating the patent expiration, it designed a new portion pack, called the Vue, with a larger form factor that would accommodate a bigger payload of ingredients. But markets can be stubborn when you ask them to switch from something they know and love to a new and untested alternative. The Vue portion pack hasn't been embraced the way the K-Cup was.

Keurig also introduced an entirely new brewing system in the summer of 2014. Built into the advanced engineering of what was dubbed Keurig 2.0 was technology that would accommodate only newly redesigned K-Cups imprinted with scanner codes that the brewer could read. Anything else—older K-Cups or unlicensed third-party K-Cup-style portion packs—simply would not brew.

To customers new to Keurig, these changes didn't much matter. But to loyal long-term users, they were an unpleasant surprise. The foundational benefit of offering a wide variety of choices played a big part in making the Keurig system so successful. That the new brewer couldn't accommodate unlicensed third-party roasts bothered many customers. Even more irritating to some was that the new brewer also couldn't accept My K-Cup, a handy reusable portion-pack adaptor for customers who wanted to buy, grind, and brew their own coffees in a Keurig machine.

From the perspective of engineering a clever solution to the patent-expiration problem, Keurig 2.0 made sense. But patent expiration wasn't really the customers' problem. To them, Keurig appeared to have suddenly gone back on its core brand promise about variety and choice. Buyers of Keurig 2.0 models couldn't use the new brewer in ways they'd enjoyed in the past.

The fallout came quickly. Reviews were unenthusiastic, often scathing. While the company told *Consumer Reports* that the scanner codes were meant to precisely control the brewing parameters for particular beverage types, *Consumer Reports* noted that they also served as a digital-rights management tool "to block you from using older or unlicensed K-Cups."[12]

Some customers took matters into their own hands, using widely shared hacks that allowed the new brewer to accept old pods and reusable adaptors. But the response to the new brewer affected sales and, ultimately, Keurig's revenues. For the first quarter of 2015, sales of brewers and accessories "plunged 23% as consumers voted against the closed coffee system with their pocketbooks," reported a *USA Today* article.[13]

By midsummer 2015, Keurig Green Mountain's stock had fallen significantly and was trading in the low 70s. CEO Brian Kelley apologized in May for having misjudged the customer base and not anticipating the reaction to the brewer changes. Said Kelley, "We were wrong . . . We underestimated the passion the consumer had for this."[14] He also announced that a fix would be made to allow the new brewer to accept My K-Cup reusable adaptors. "It was a nice convenience for a lot of our very, very loyal and heavy users . . . We shouldn't have taken it away. We did, [and now] we're bringing it back."[15]

Certainly, it was commendable of Kelley to apologize on Keurig Green Mountains' behalf. But what I take away from these difficulties is the lesson that sustaining balance among the three boxes over time is an unending challenge—a journey, not a discrete event. Keurig 2.0 was at heart a Box 1 response since its dominant goal seems to have been to protect the razor-and-blades model from third-party encroachments. But that created a conflict with one of Keurig's important brand promises. Loyal customers—the ones who love your product the most—always react badly when you start subtracting perceived value. At the very least, you should offer them some clearly superior benefit that more than compensates for what's been lost. Based on the market reaction, that didn't happen in this case.

As of this writing, Keurig is readying for its next date with destiny—the launch of its new cold-beverage system, Keurig Kold. According to an article in the *Boston Globe*, the brewer is expected to retail for around $200 and use K-Cup pods, each containing a complete recipe (including carbonation) for an eight-ounce cold beverage.[16] The *Globe* article quoted an analyst, Brian Holland, who said the new product "will be the biggest test yet for [KGM's] ability to exist in the consumer's mind as more than just a coffee company. They have a lot riding on this cold product."

That is true, of course. But for Box 3, the heart of the challenge is *always* to succeed when a lot is riding on what it creates.

In the next chapter, we turn to Box 2. The dominant Box 2 activity is to selectively forget old ideas, practices, processes, systems, and mind-sets—in short, anything that acts as a barrier to nonlinear innovations. In practical terms, Box 2 is also where you put in place the conditions most likely to favor planned opportunism, so that no matter what the future brings, you have built the skills, insights, structures, and attitudes you will need to respond resiliently.

The ultimate test of a Box 3 culture is whether it can sustain itself over the decades. I believe sustainability depends to a great extent on how disciplined and committed an organization is when it comes to Box 2 behavior. For that reason, Box 2 is the most indispensable and most challenging component of the Three-Box Solution. It's also worth noting that the lack of strong Box 2 capabilities will inevitably cause an organization to become mired in the past and lose its way. In chapter 3, we will look at how IBM developed an ambitious Box 2 strategy as a way of rejuvenating its Box 3 future.

Takeaways

- *Box 3 innovation is a painstaking process of experimentation that calls for patient leadership.* If Keurig's outside investors had not been willing to show the necessary patience through frustrating rounds of trial and error, Keurig might never have reached its consumer-market breakthrough.

- *Your best opportunities may include a business model that relies on alliances with other businesses.* Keurig's model intertwined its fate with that of independent coffee roasters. As Keurig grew, it offered roasters a way to spread their brand identities and increase the revenue per pound of their roasts. That, in turn, strengthened Keurig's brand and value proposition.

- *The right combination of depth and breadth adds creative potential to anyone's skill set.* As Kevin Sullivan's hiring profile for engineers shows, people who combine deep specialization with a broad understanding of how their work fits into the larger scheme of things are able to see opportunities and help solve problems in adjacent areas. This approach would likely add value to almost any business discipline in any type of organization.

- *Learning always precedes innovation.* Box 3 ventures are filled with uncertainty and powered by experimentation. Risks should be embraced as learning opportunities. But learning should focus above all else on resolving uncertainty and reducing risk by testing critical assumptions.

- *Placing smaller bets before bigger bets is the best way of limiting investments when the volume of risk is highest and the amount of certainty is lowest.* Doing this is especially important in cases where your target market is embryonic.

- *It is important to create a Box 3 culture in your organization.* In fact, this is the main imperative behind the practice of *planned opportunism*—preparing for the future even when you can't reliably predict it. Build the new skills, structures, and attitudes that will make nonlinear Box 3 thinking a habit.

TOOLS

Tool 1: Generate Box 3 Ideas

Refer to your answers to tool 2 in chapter 1. Identify new Box 3 business models your company could create to exploit two or more nonlinear changes. What innovative product or service concepts can you develop either to access currently unserved parts of the market or to create entirely new markets?

After brainstorming and identifying several Box 3 ideas, using a scale of 1 to 5, rate each Box 3 idea on two dimensions:

- *Attractiveness of the idea.* The attractiveness of an idea depends on the size of the addressable market, future growth, and so on. This is not a market research exercise; simply use rough estimates (1 = not attractive, 5 = highly attractive).

- *Feasibility.* Feasibility is defined as your ability to capture the opportunity. Typical factors you may want to consider include your existing competencies and capabilities, how contested the market is, barriers to adoption, and so on (1 = not feasible, 5 = highly feasible).

Add the score for *attractiveness of the idea* and the score for *feasibility* to obtain a *total score* for each Box 3 idea.

The Box 3 idea with the highest score is the most attractive idea. Start executing it with the tool below.

Tool 2: Execute a Box 3 Idea

- What skill sets and competencies are needed for the Box 3 project? Which are available in-house? For which do you have to make external hires? Similar to Keurig, *new* Box 3 capabilities should be built in a *dedicated team* that is distinct and separate from the *performance engine*.

- Identify performance engine assets that could provide the Box 3 project with a competitive advantage so compelling it could make or break the chance of success for the Box 3 idea. This discussion establishes what the dedicated team must borrow from the performance engine. Executing a Box 3 project is about knowing how to *separate* it from the performance engine, while *coexisting* with the performance engine.

- Conflicts are inevitable when the Box 3 project borrows assets from the performance engine. The goal is not to eliminate conflicts but to manage them. What conflicts will naturally arise at operational points of interaction between the performance engine and the Box 3 project in your organization? Scarce resources? Different standards? Different notions of what is best for the corporation as a whole? Jealousy that the dedicated team is more valued? What would be the best methods to resolve these conflicts?

- There are two types of acceptable outcomes in a Box 3 innovation project: (a) a success and (b) a failure that comes as quickly and inexpensively as possible. The most undesirable outcome is a long, expensive, and painful failure. Therefore, as the Box 3 project moves forward, you want to be sure that you spend a little to learn a lot. To accomplish this, you must *test the most critical assumptions as early and as inexpensively as possible.* A cross-functional team should identify the assumptions that are inherent in scaling up the Box 3 initiative into a successful business. Be as specific as possible. Consider the following generic types of assumptions:

- Have you correctly understood the customer problem, independent of the solution?

- Will your business-model solution address the customer problem?

- What is the size of the addressable market?

- What price point will unlock the market?

- How many units will you get at your target price?

- Do you have the technologies that are required to find the solution?

- Do you know the optimal manufacturing architecture to make the product?

- How well have you estimated your costs?

- Do you have the capabilities to execute and scale up?

- Have you planned the right go-to-market approach?

- Do you know the appropriate model to provide customer service postsale?

- Who are your competitors today?

- Who else will enter the market?

- How vigorously will the new entrants pursue the market?

- How will competitors' actions affect demand for your product?

Now identify critical assumptions. Using a scale of 1 to 5, rate each of the assumptions on its degree of uncertainty (1 = certain, 5 = wild guess) and the degree of consequence if you are wrong

(1 = minor, 5 = severe). The assumptions with the highest total score are the most critical–the ones you should test first. What low-cost experiments can you design to test the critical assumptions?

· Executing a Box 3 project is about knowing how to run a *disciplined experiment*. Your ability to learn faster than your competition is your only sustainable competitive advantage. The best way to deliver financial results in Box 3 is not to focus on short-term financial criteria. Instead, you should use leading indicators to evaluate Box 3 experiments. The leading indicators provide signals about resolving the critical assumptions. That ultimately leads to financial success. What should be the performance appraisal criteria for the specific Box 3 idea your company is undertaking?

3

Forget the Past

Box 2 is where obstacles to the Box 3 future go to die. As I briefly touched on in chapter 1, Box 2's most transformative role is to help organizations shake free of the inhibiting ideas and structures that have arisen around past successes. As one executive, Hylke Faber, the founder of Constancee, told me, "As soon as I find the courage to say good-bye to a past that no longer serves—not looking back, flexing my Box 2 muscles—I'm ready to take my first step into my new future. Then the magic of Box 3 begins."

Indeed, there is really nothing quite so powerful as an entrenched set of obsolete values and practices. They can easily come to seem as immutable as the laws of physics. But where the laws of physics are generally helpful, the dominance of the past has the ability to freeze time and enforce inertia.

Consider the parable of the four monkeys, which I first heard from one of my colleagues.[1]

Four monkeys sit together at the foot of a coconut palm tree. Tired of waiting for a coconut to fall, one of the monkeys decides to climb the tree and pick some. However, after nearly reaching the top, he receives an electric shock and scampers back to the ground. The other monkeys are alarmed and agitated. The first monkey tries again, with the same result. Then, one by one, the other monkeys decide to see for themselves, and the tree likewise shocks them before they can reach the height of the coconuts. It doesn't take long for the monkeys to understand that *it is very dangerous to climb the tree*. Thus, when it comes to coconut trees, they learn from experience that the only acceptable business model is to wait for gravity, rather than monkey initiative, to deliver the coconuts.

The four monkeys encode this understanding in their organizational policies, employee handbooks, training programs, performance metrics, and organizational structures. The understanding becomes an orthodoxy. The monkeys stop questioning why climbing the coconut palm is a bad idea.

Eventually, the four monkeys are transferred to another tree, one that would not administer a shock if only they dared to climb it. But they don't. Despite a nonlinear change in circumstances, the monkeys behave exactly as they were conditioned to do by their previous environment. They have carried the experience of electric shock with them to the new tree. At some point, management removes one of the four monkeys and replaces it with a new monkey, one whose past does not include being shocked by a coconut tree. As he begins to climb the tree to retrieve a coconut, the other monkeys pull him down. Again and again, the new monkey starts climbing, but the other three intervene. They explain to this maverick thinker that it is impermissible even to attempt to climb the tree. Gravity is the only acceptable business model.

"So you can only wait?" asks the new monkey.

"What we do is hope for a windy day that will loosen the tree's hold on the coconuts," says one of the others.

Eventually, the new monkey accepts, without quite knowing why, that climbing the tree is dangerous and not allowed. Even though he has never experienced a shock, he comes to understand that the tree isn't meant to be climbed and any attempt to do so will be met by determined opposition. Thus can a new monkey with different ideas and past experiences be socialized to adopt old ideas.

One by one, each of the original monkeys is replaced. And all of the new monkeys learn, without ever receiving a shock, that it is dangerous to climb the coconut tree. This is how old logic, which has outlived the circumstances that created it, persists even when nonlinear change brings new, potentially attractive opportunities. But those opportunities are lost because the past was allowed to become too powerful.

For that reason, it is important for organizations to develop the discipline of *selectively forgetting* whatever has outlived its contemporary usefulness or, if it still has value to the Box 1 business, devising ways of insulating Box 3 from its inhibiting effects.

Box 2 Hallmark Principles and Behaviors

One Box 2 responsibility is to prune lines of business that no longer fit the company's strategy. For instance, GE took bold Box 2 action in April 2015 when it announced it would sell off most of the assets of its GE Capital unit to focus on its high-tech industrial businesses. The company expected to reap $26.5 billion from the sale of its real estate assets alone, cash that could fund Box 3 initiatives in health care, energy, and transportation. Fast-tracking GE Capital had been the right Box 1 move for GE in the 1980s and '90s; by 2000, financial services provided more than half the company's revenue. But economic and societal changes in the new millennium caused GE to rethink its priorities—a different company for a different time.

In his public announcement, chair and CEO Jeff Immelt said that in considering the move, GE's board and management team "asked . . . some key questions: What is going on in the world? Is this the right

Letting Go of the Wrong Future

Tata Consultancy Services (TCS)—part of the Tata Group, one of India's largest and most respected businesses—had evolved from being one of a half dozen of India's pioneering IT outsourcing providers into the clear leader in the global IT services field, with about three hundred thousand employees. Despite a global slowdown in the North American and European outsourcing markets, TCS doubled its revenues—$6 billion to $12 billion—from 2010 to 2014. At a market cap of $70 billion, it had become India's most valuable company.

TCS's transformation was enabled by bold Box 2 actions. For instance, in the first few years of the new millennium, the company became quite successful in the thriving sector of offshore call centers. Business process outsourcing was a high-growth industry, and call centers were in particularly high demand. And yet, after only a couple of years, TCS abruptly decided to discontinue its call-center service. It did so not because the business wasn't growing and prospering, but because company leaders saw that developing the competencies necessary to operate an exceptionally successful call center had begun to take TCS in an unwanted direction.

Experience showed that the average tenure of a call-center operator ranged from three months to a year, according to TCS's former chief executive

time? Is this good for customers and investors? What will GE look like going forward?"[2] In order to pursue its future, GE realized it had to selectively forget the past, even one that had proved very profitable. (See the sidebar, "Letting Go of the Wrong Future," about a seemingly counterintuitive divestiture by Tata Consultancy Services, one of India's largest technology businesses.)

P&G has likewise embarked on a bold divestiture strategy with the aim of focusing management attention on a smaller number of higher-growth core brands. For example, in July 2015 it announced the sale of forty-three of its beauty brands to Coty Inc.[4] The Coty deal and officer, S. Ramadorai (known as Ram). This caused enormous work-force churn and intensely drained management energy, as TCS cycled as many as a half-million workers through the company annually. More relevant to TCS's future was that the call-center business, while profit-able, wasn't strategic to customers; rather, it was a way for the com-pany to bring down costs in areas it regarded as outside its core.

Moreover, TCS wanted its mission to evolve toward providing custom-ers with greater strategic value. Sales revenue per employee tended to be higher for higher value-added services, so by focusing on those services, TCS could significantly grow the top line with a smaller, more stable workforce. Explained Ram, "We made a very conscious decision to say [call-center work was] not the capability we wanted to build. It was not where we wanted to be because the value-add was very low. So we said, 'Let's take a chance and move away from the call-center business.'"[3]

The work of sustaining a low-value-added call-center operation would drain so much enterprise energy, focus, capital, and ingenuity that the evolu-tion toward developing more-strategic offerings would very likely be derailed. The move to exit an area of rapidly growing demand was highly unusual, but TCS felt that the call-center operation was the wrong future to pursue.

other divestitures are part of P&G's plan to get rid of as many as a hundred brands in order to free up both capital and bandwidth to manage the growth of just ten product lines.

Divestitures such as these, done as part of a Box 2 portfolio-management strategy, can unburden your organization of assets that (1) have diminishing value, (2) demand management attention that outweighs the revenues they produce, and (3) might attract a good price from an outside buyer. But divestitures are often difficult and challenging to execute. They raise an assortment of internal anxiet-ies and market concerns, and they require the active commitment of powerful executives. Thus, even though divestitures create liquidity that can be invested in future growth, there are other Box 2 levers that can have a more direct positive effect on Box 3 innovation.

In this chapter, I focus mainly on measures that change the way people work, manage, and *think* across lines of business at different stages of development, because as hard as it can be to divest tangible business assets, it is harder still to take the knife to the less obvious but more insidious menace of organizational memory.

Managers running the Box 1 performance engine develop a *dominant logic* consisting of mind-sets built out of what they have experienced in the past.[5] Dominant logic becomes further embedded in systems, structures, processes, and cultures that are self-perpetuating. Dominant logic is especially powerful in companies that tend to promote from within and to have homogeneous cultures, strong socialization mechanisms, and a long track record of success. Such deeply rooted memory may be great for preservation (Box 1), but if it is not tamed sufficiently (Box 2), it gets in the way of creation (Box 3). That's why all Box 3 initiatives really begin in Box 2. Bottom line: *before you can create, you must forget.*

Organizations that lack a Box 2 discipline tend to behave like the four monkeys; they do not notice that many entrenched mind-sets have lost relevance in changing circumstances and are putting their futures in jeopardy. The good news is that organizations can master Box 2 as an instrument for keeping the past, present, and future in balance.

IBM's Fall from Grace

During most of the last quarter of the twentieth century, IBM was a highly disciplined Box 1 paragon. It became the go-to provider of enterprise information technology—hardware, software, and systems integration—for large and midsize businesses. Technology, being both expensive and complicated, was always a risky purchase. The chief information officers (CIOs) responsible for making buying decisions suffered from famously high turnover—their average tenure during the 1990s was scarcely more than two years—and so they highly valued IBM's reputation for quality and dependability. It was seen as the safe choice for under-the-gun CIOs. As the saying at the time went, "Nobody ever got fired for buying Big Blue."

IBM feasted on its role as the industry's most respected incumbent. CIOs who kept their jobs while buying IBM technologies could think of themselves as smart, and IBM grew comfortable with its standing as the preeminent brand in enterprise computing.

However, two nonlinear shifts threatened IBM's dominance:

- *Personal computing.* By the mid-1980s, PCs, initially seen as toys for hobbyists, began to pervade businesses. The irony was that IBM had played a pivotal role (along with Bill Gates's little start-up, Microsoft) in legitimizing PCs as business tools. Once PCs rapidly increased their power and utility (thanks to Moore's Law and new business software applications) and were connected to client/server networks, it was thought to be only a matter of time before sales of IBM's ubiquitous mainframe and midrange systems would decline.[6]

- *The internet and web.* The second, more powerful shift was, of course, the internet and especially the hyperlinking World Wide Web. Any computer anywhere in the world was able to interact with any other that had an internet connection. Businesses could overflow their traditional boundaries, discovering the value of direct and measurable customer interactions, which could be captured and analyzed. Soon enough, it became possible to design virtual processes and workplaces. The usual entry barriers for competing in many industries were either lowered or vanished entirely, as Amazon showed by becoming a successful book retailer without carrying any book inventory.

Though separated by more than a decade, these two nonlinear developments opened the eyes of businesses to the possibility of escaping the trap of proprietary technologies and to the equally appealing idea that the web might become a virtual operating system over which computing capabilities and applications—all built around standard protocols—could be acquired efficiently and cheaply, to be paid for as they were consumed in the manner of a utility. Today, this idea is called "the cloud."[7]

Three Traps

While there were many within IBM who clearly understood the implications of both nonlinear shifts, their insights had difficulty penetrating the entrenched logic of the past. The dominant logic of the past exerts its hold on business cultures and practices in three distinctive but tightly interlocking ways. I think of their dynamic effects as traps that snare the unprepared. All three have common origins in mind-sets that focus excessively on past values, behavior, and beliefs.

The Complacency Trap

Current success conditions a business to suppose that securing the future requires nothing more than repeating what it did to succeed in the past. This is the *complacency trap*. Complacency shrouds the future in a fog of misplaced confidence, hiding from view a clear understanding of the extent to which the world is changing around you.

IBM's extraordinary success driving revenues in its Box 1 mainframe business masked difficulties to come. Rather than face up to looming threats to the mainframe business, IBM applied temporary patches. One such patch was to change the revenue model from leasing mainframes to selling them outright.[8] This produced a pleasing surge in near-term revenues that postponed IBM's day of reckoning.

The loyalty of successful organizations to the past is often so potent that they become quite ingenious at ignoring the onset of fatigue in the Box 1 business. Instead of building the future day by day, IBM prolonged its past with what amounted to an accounting change. The resulting years-long period of bolstered revenues made it easy for the company to think that *everything was just fine*—four words that fairly summarize complacency.

Another way to understand how IBM fell into the complacency trap is that the company's continuing Box 1 profitability delayed development of a sense of urgency that might have motivated a more prescient Box 2 judgment: that it was important to invest aggressively in the new enterprise model of client/server computing.

This is the dark side of success. No matter the industry or company, each great innovation spawns a steady accumulation of Box 1–based structures, processes, and attitudes of the kind that blinded IBM to its predicament. IBM mainframes were not simply smart machines; they were smart machines that over the years had created at customer work sites whole new layers of enterprise management that had never existed before.

Mainframe computers were island fortresses, secured and operated by a newly empowered IT function and inaccessible, except through IT proxies, to the rest of the enterprise. If a technology can embody a governing philosophy, the mainframe's philosophy was exactly opposite that of the open, accessible internet that was yet to appear. Even before the internet emerged as a business tool, there were pitched battles within almost every company about making valuable mainframe data accessible to and usable by employees with networked PCs. This increasingly loud demand clashed with the mind-set of IBM's IT customers, who saw their mission as protecting the security and integrity of corporate data: allowing liberal access would lead to data corruption and to proliferating unreliable versions of the "truth."

In fact, customers can play an important role in deepening a complacency trap. IBM had collaborated with its customers in creating what became an entrenched system of governance for computerized organizations. That system's structures and attitudes were a self-reinforcing feedback loop amplified by IBM's large-enterprise customers.

Ultimately, a more modern version of the mainframe emerged and made peace with the rest of the IT infrastructure. Today's version powers big data analytics and other applications in many large enterprises. But in the IBM of the 1990s, mainframes cast a long shadow over the emergent model of more open, democratized network computing.

The Cannibalization Trap

The cannibalization trap persuades leaders that new business models based on nonlinear ideas will jeopardize the firm's present prosperity. So, like antibodies attacking an invading virus, they protect the Box 1 business by resisting ideas that don't conform to models of the past.

At its heart, the fear of cannibalization reflects a wish to keep the world from changing. It is perhaps easy to understand that wish, but it's much harder to excuse it. The glib answer to those who suffer from this fear is to remind them that change is inevitable and the world will change either with them or without them. When a business allows worries about cannibalization to interfere with its strategy, it has overinvested in its past and is doomed to undermine its future.

Cannibalization is typically understood—and feared—as a near-term threat. As foresighted as IBM was in developing its personal computer in the early 1980s, forces marshaled within the company to protect the legacy business. Those who feared the PC believed it had the potential to threaten the mainframe computing model, perhaps by feeding the growing appetite to liberate enterprise data or by diverting attention and investment away from the company's dominant business.

People who fear new technology are usually more right than wrong about its potential to supersede legacy products. The truth is, every Box 1 business has reason to fear, sometimes even hate, whatever shiny new thing is being launched. When Steve Jobs gave a big push to the Macintosh launch toward the end of his first stint at Apple, the group in charge of the incumbent Apple II felt threatened and undercut. It was as if cofounder Jobs had sponsored an insurrection.[9]

In reality, however, cannibalization should be understood as a long-term benefit. The new Apple Macintosh embodied features that soon enough would make its predecessors obsolete. If Apple hadn't moved quickly, a competitor—maybe even IBM—would have filled the vacuum. Given its history, IBM's embrace of microcomputing was unexpected. But it quickly set the standard for PCs and legitimized them as tools for both home and business users. While IBM's marketing of the PC initially tilted toward home users, the real revenue bonanza came from businesses. Suddenly, at least part of IBM had reason to root for client/server computing. No matter what anyone in the mainframe business thought about it, the client/server model had the shine of inevitability.

So, while companies must take the fear of cannibalization seriously as a problem to manage, it can't become a reason not to act with foresight when new nonlinear strategies or business models present an opportunity.

The Competency Trap

The competency trap arises when positive results in the current core business encourage the organization to invest mainly in Box 1 competencies and provide little incentive for investing in new and future-oriented competencies. In established companies built around a spectacular success, such as IBM's industry-defining mainframe computers, it is natural to want to create a workforce whose skills dominantly reflect the legacy success. But a competency trap is a double-edged sword. IBM's investments in Box 1 competencies helped its mainframe business. But Box 1 logic asks, *why invest in skills not vital to the company's current profitability?* That is why Box 2 is necessary.

IBM eventually recognized that the dominant computing model it had exploited to achieve such great success was changing. Yet, despite having made significant investments in a robust R&D function, it was having chronic difficulty incubating new ventures. It struggled to find what IBM insiders called "The Next Big Thing."[10] The organization appeared to have succumbed to a "four monkeys" value system.

Believing that there were indeed systemic problems, then-CEO Louis V. Gerstner commissioned an internal inquiry to identify root causes. The inquiry, led by Bruce Harreld, IBM's head of corporate strategy, confirmed Gerstner's fears. Looking at a number of recent examples of flawed new-business incubation, Harreld's team concluded that the company's dominant Box 1 systems, structures, processes, and culture had:

- Created a powerful bias for near-term results.

- Encouraged a focus on existing customers and offerings to the extent that new technologies and nonlinear trends were either underestimated or escaped detection entirely.

- Burdened new businesses with unreasonably high performance goals—especially damaging to ventures that targeted newer, riskier, but often more promising markets.

- Motivated an unimaginative approach to market analysis that impaired the company's ability to understand the sorts of "embryonic markets" most likely to spawn nonlinear Box 3 ideas.

- Interfered with development of the skills necessary to adaptively transition a new business through its emergent and growth stages until it finally became an established enterprise.

- Caused assorted failures of execution, many owing to the inflexibility of Box 1–driven organizational structures, which leaders of new ventures "were expected to rise above . . . Voicing concerns over [such challenges], even when they were major barriers to new business initiatives, was seen as a sign of weakness."[11]

What the report didn't say is important to note. IBM's problem was not caused by a lack of research competency. On the contrary, its workforce possessed at least some expertise in a wide array of disciplines and technologies. Among its research projects were some that were quite promising and others that were highly speculative, unproven, and obscure. But for all the reasons listed, even ideas that managed to get traction were being ineptly developed and executed. What IBM needed was a well-designed process for enabling, supporting, and rewarding its maverick monkeys and likewise for managing new ventures onward through their developmental stages.

Such a process typically should incorporate a range of structural, cultural, and leadership remedies. At IBM—first under Gerstner and later Sam Palmisano—these distinctive remedies came together under the emerging business opportunities (EBO) framework, which created new structures, changes to the buttoned-down IBM culture, and more versatile and adaptive leadership behavior.

Box 2 Remedies

Bringing in Lou Gerstner, with his outsider perspective—he came to IBM in 1993 from RJR Nabisco, the first CEO not promoted from within the ranks of company executives—proved to have been a significant Box 2 move. Gerstner's background was mostly in business-to-consumer (B2C) businesses, including American Express. Although his initial charge was to break up IBM and sell off its pieces, he heeded the advice of customers and kept the company together. By his own example, he made IBM more customer-centric, forcing its culture to behave with greater humility—recognizing it had something to learn from customers—and to throw off its smug self-certainty. Gerstner led IBM's transformation from a hardware and software company at its core to, instead, a service provider. Its new mission was to help customers migrate from the old, closed world of enterprise mainframes to the open, nonproprietary world of networked computers and, ultimately, the internet—a world where customers' enterprise architectures, processes, and commercial activities could be flexibly reconfigured as needed.

By the end of the 1990s, Gerstner had repaired IBM's complacent Box 1 performance, getting the company out of its unprecedented run of money-losing quarters. Not surprisingly, however, a by-product of the urgent emphasis on Box 1 produced a redoubled focus on near-term execution. That inevitably tempted leaders of Box 1 business units to undervalue investments in Box 3 projects. To successfully create the future, Gerstner had to start with a Box 2 action.

Beginning with the conclusions of Harreld's report, he ordered up a project to develop a broad institutional solution that would address every aspect of developing an emerging business—from the germ of an idea to experimentation and incubation, then on to growth and mature revenue performance. EBOs would be a way of escaping the past. Key to the EBO framework would be the recognition that ventures at different stages of development require different strategies, management approaches, and performance-measurement criteria.

Box 2 is really about enhancing the possibility of creating divergent futures. All told, under Gerstner (who retired in 2002) and Palmisano (who retired in 2012), one measure alone shows a business that was not just patched up but also thoroughly renovated. Between 1993 and 2012, IBM's stock price went from $13 to $193 (14 percent annual compounded growth in market capitalization over a twenty-year period), and the company caught up with the real-time pace of change in the ways its customers—and *their* customers—were doing business.

Later, we'll take a look at EBOs through the lens of IBM's pervasive computing business. The pervasive computing unit had been among the examples singled out in Harreld's report on missed opportunities. The unit's unfulfilled potential made it a promising laboratory in which to test the ideas behind the EBO approach. With the aim of changing the unit's fortunes, IBM rolled it into the EBO framework in early 2000. It ultimately went on to become one of the most successful EBOs IBM had incubated.

Starting in 1993, IBM pursued numerous disparate research initiatives related to a concept that came to be called "pervasive computing," also known as Tier 0 (where, in IBM's taxonomy, Tiers 3, 2, and 1 were mainframe, midrange, and personal computers, respectively). The objective of these projects was to investigate and develop new technologies based on the idea that internet commerce would rapidly spread beyond computers to other devices, from cell phones and PDAs to cars, kitchen appliances, and other network-addressable objects—hence, the name "pervasive computing."[12] A perfect present-day example is the networked E-ZPass transponder in cars that automatically debits the cost of highway tolls from drivers' bank accounts.

In its initial years, the pervasive computing unit struggled to get traction because the nonlinear opportunity was assigned to many siloed Box 1 businesses, which applied a range of past-based development approaches—the typical four-monkeys problem. Senior management, persuaded that Tier 0 held great potential as a business opportunity, wanted to unify and coordinate the various projects under a single EBO umbrella.

The EBO process sought to improve IBM's track record for launching new businesses by developing a more start-up–friendly structure as well as a separate set of practices in the areas of organization, leadership/management, resource allocation, strategy development, and performance measurement and motivation.

It is worth stressing again that the goal of Box 2 remedies is not to eradicate Box 1 skills and values, which continue to power the organization's performance engine, but rather to create protective structures and alternative competencies that allow nonlinear Box 3 innovations to flourish.

Organization and Leadership

The first principle of the EBO framework was to explicitly recognize that emerging ventures have unique requirements. They need protection and insulation from the rules that govern Box 1 businesses. In their early stages, they thrive on the luxury of patience. Therefore, they must be organized for learning, not earning. They take a structural form that favors a clean-slate (meaning unburdened by the inhibiting past) mind-set and an operational commitment to iterative experimentation. It is imperative to forget the past when technologies are new, nonlinear, and untested and when markets, like those that pervasive computing unit was investigating, are undefined and still evolving. As the pervasive unit's experience demonstrated, forcing an embryonic venture to move too quickly into an embryonic market is damaging.

Instead of placing the pervasive computing unit under the control of one of the division presidents in charge of the performance engine, it was assigned to a dedicated team that reported directly to vice chairman John Thompson. Thompson had a reputation within IBM for successfully shepherding challenging projects. The move protected the pervasive unit from the bottom-line pressures of Box 1. (Had each new monkey in the parable not been brainwashed by the existing organization, the monkeys would have behaved differently.)

Gerstner (and later Palmisano) handpicked EBO leaders based on two criteria: they needed to be change agents able to challenge IBM's orthodoxies and, at the same time, capable of leveraging the core assets of Box 1 businesses. After all, pervasive computing was a "white space" opportunity that required the resources and capabilities of many IBM business units; it could not be executed by any one business unit.

Gerstner recruited twenty-one-year IBM veteran Rodney Adkins to take over the pervasive computing unit in the summer of 2001. He saw in Adkins a solid technologist, risk taker, and gifted leader, one with a high profile across the company; he most recently had turned around IBM's web server business. In a company like IBM, the choice of unit leaders is loaded with significance. Adkins recalled that IBM "picked some of the best leaders in the company to take charge of EBOs, which sent a strong message to the organization that we were serious about the EBO program. Top talent is always in short supply. Lou [Gerstner] was personally involved in appointing EBO leaders. Otherwise, the core business will not let go of their best people." And it was important that the top talent was willing to take the plunge.

Adkins said he had some reservations at the time about leaving his job running a highly successful business, one that amounted to "a large segment of the company's business." But he was persuaded in conversations with senior leadership that IBM "was making a very real commitment to the pervasive unit. It just spoke volumes."

Adkins's appointment signaled, both internally and to the market-place, that IBM's commitment to the pervasive computing unit was genuine and long term. And because Adkins was familiar with the performance engine's ins and outs, he was better able to command resources and talent within the company as needed. Sooner or later, every EBO would need to draw on IBM's deep functional skills and expertise. Whereas an outsider would have had to build trust and confidence first before being able to effectively borrow from the performance engine, the entrenched Box 1 culture would have a harder time saying no to leaders with heavyweight clout.

It is true that long-tenured employees are more likely to carry forward the baggage of past successes. To guard against that problem, Gerstner and Palmisano scouted and identified insiders who were willing to embrace change. The EBO program was further safeguarded against the weight of past baggage through its architecture—its structure, process, and management culture. Additionally, Thompson evangelized the need to selectively forget the past: "There were people in the organization who didn't like [the EBO], who were too turfy. So I had to keep preaching the story and occasionally make an example by putting someone in the doghouse."[13] Gerstner echoed a similar sentiment: "IBM's number one issue is revenue growth. General managers have to understand that they won't be successful if they focus only on their core businesses."[14]

Leaders in emerging businesses have some duties that are essential to successful incubation. They must change the organization's culture by changing its narrative from the old one, created by the legacy success, to an alternative that encompasses important new ideas and directions.

In the near term, the objective is to persuade the organization as a whole to accept—rather than attack with antibodies—the emergence of a potentially powerful successor growing around the nonlinear innovation at the core of the EBO. The new narrative, while it won't entirely replace the old one, is a potent lever for engineering long-term change. And it is the job of leaders to articulate it with unmistakable vividness and conviction. (For a look at how CEO Satya Nadella is changing the narrative at Microsoft, see the sidebar, "Revitalizing Microsoft.")

What does it mean to change the narrative? In Gerstner's early tenure at IBM, one of the first things he noticed was that senior executives were accustomed to making brief cameo appearances at IBM-hosted customer events and then disappearing without bothering to spend time actually engaging with the customers, creating the impression that the executives had better things to do with their time. Gerstner, who liked nothing more than to pick customers' brains, was appalled. As recalled by Bill Etherington, former general manager of IBM Canada, when Gerstner learned of an upcoming two-day IBM conference for three hundred North American CIOs, he told his executive staff, "These are your best customers . . . I'm going to the whole conference. I'll be there the first night. I'll have dinner with them. I'll have breakfast with them. I'll have lunch with them. And any IBM executive who wants to attend will stay for the whole two days."[18]

During the conference, said Etherington, Gerstner "opened a dialogue with the customers and he started to single IBM executives out. 'This executive will fix that and get back to you this afternoon.' It was unheard of—'The CEO's siding with the customers!' That was like a rocket through the company."[19]

Changing a culture is never quick or easy. Clearly, this is one area where visible leadership like Gerstner's is indispensable when trying to plant the seeds for a new culture by changing the narrative. Entrenched cultures build ardent, reflexive loyalties. Sometimes, there is nothing like "a rocket through the company" to get people's attention.

Revitalizing Microsoft

Microsoft's meteoric growth, built on the foundation of the MS-DOS operating system, occurred hand in glove with the rising utility of microcomputers. During its early years, Microsoft shrewdly filled key capabilities gaps for PC users with offerings like the bundled Microsoft Office suite of tools. Of course, part of Microsoft Office's success lay in its superior integration with MS-DOS and, later, Windows and its successor operating systems.

To maximize that advantage, Microsoft pressured computer makers to bundle its products—including Office and, eventually, its Internet Explorer browser—along with the operating system. PC makers may have chafed at the pressure, but they knew Microsoft's applications were giving customers compelling reasons to buy computers. The fortunes of Microsoft and the PC manufacturers were intertwined. By the early 1990s, Microsoft's Box 1 business—Windows-powered PCs—dominated the market.

In subsequent years, however, Microsoft seemed to lose its way. As Bill Gates famously admitted in his book *The Road Ahead*, he and Microsoft were caught flat-footed by the swift emergence of the internet as a new computing platform and by the web browser as its de facto operating system. Hard as Microsoft tried to catch up, Internet Explorer established a pattern characterized by eleventh-hour efforts to remain relevant as the world changed around it. Silicon Valley start-ups were achieving the breakthroughs and setting the pace.

Why would an extraordinarily successful organization lose its ability to anticipate the future? Because *future weaknesses are embedded in current strengths.* Box 3 innovations begin with Box 2 remedies. But Microsoft was unable to grasp early enough the weak signal that PC sales would decline once users embraced smaller, more convenient computing platforms. Because PCs were the foundation of its success, forgetting became a major challenge.

Since 2000, Microsoft has struggled to compete in almost every emerging technology area: search, digital music, smartphones and other mobile platforms, cloud computing, social networking, and the nimble app-develop-ment techniques that flourish in social networks. Instead, it offered me-too versions of devices that did not materially improve on others' innovations. Now the company is on the cusp of an existential tipping point similar in some respects to the one IBM faced in the 1990s.

Like IBM, Microsoft wasn't blind to emergent technologies. But in terms of Box 2, exceptionally successful companies must overcome *extra* drag in order to properly incubate and exploit new nonlinear ideas, whereas Silicon Valley start-ups, unencumbered by drag, move more quickly and adaptively.

Under new CEO Nadella, Microsoft is making big Box 2 strides. In April 2014, just two months after taking the helm, Nadella announced Microsoft would give away its Windows operating system to manufacturers of smart-phones and tablets, in order to motivate more developers to create apps and services for the Microsoft platform on mobile devices. This is a departure from Microsoft's founding tenet that software should be paid for. But it clears needed space for Nadella's vision that Microsoft must thrive in the world of "mobile first, cloud first."[15]

Nadella is changing the narrative in other ways:

- He has turned once-contentious relationships (with Oracle, for instance) into cooperative ventures—and sometimes partnerships—anticipating that such alliances might lead to better-performing Microsoft products.

- In a move he called "difficult, but necessary," he trimmed eighteen thousand jobs.[16]

- He is breaking down Microsoft silos that have stifled Box 3 initiatives, encouraging, for example, closer collaboration between researchers and product engineers.

(continued)

(*continued*)

- Known for his low tolerance of new products with "glitches" (such as those that plagued the Surface tablet), he has set the bar higher throughout the organization.

- In his communications across the company, he has repeatedly urged employees to embrace innovation, not tradition.

"Our ambitions are bold, and so must be our desire to change and evolve our culture," Nadella wrote on Microsoft.com. "Nothing is off the table in how we think about shifting our culture to deliver on this core strategy. Organizations will change. Job responsibilities will evolve. New partnerships will be formed. Tired traditions will be questioned. Our priorities will be adjusted. New skills will be built. New ideas will be heard. New hires will be made. Processes will be simplified. And if you want to thrive at Microsoft and make a world impact, you and your team must add numerous more changes to this list that you will be enthusiastic about driving."[17]

This new narrative at Microsoft is paying off. Innovations launched under Nadella's leadership, such as HoloLens (computerized "smart glasses"), a touch version of Microsoft Office, and Skype Translator (a real-time language translation tool), are generating the kind of excitement that used to be reserved for Apple wares.

In fact, the leader of any other type of institution should learn the value of firing a rocket now and then. For example, from the start of his papacy, Pope Francis has been changing the narrative of the Catholic Church by loudly and publicly challenging the dominant logic of its entrenched old guard. He has turned the church's culture in the direction of tolerance, openness, and communication. He has injected new vitality by emphasizing humility and pastoral service over ceremonial pomp and rigid enforcement of doctrine. Importantly, he has made examples of certain vocal, highly visible opponents of his reforms, demoting them from exalted Vatican positions to more humble outposts—the papal equivalent of the doghouse.

Strategy Development and Resource Allocation

In Box 1 businesses, strategy changes in linear ways and within such familiar parameters as relatively stable markets, an existing customer base with established, well-understood needs, and a business model that operates efficiently through time-tested systems and processes. But Box 3 strategy development is very different. The first step in creating a new strategy process is a Box 2 action: abandon the traditional practice.

Once the pervasive computing unit was absorbed into the EBO process, it adopted an operational structure that was largely independent of standard Box 1 expectations. Instead, the venture was scaled more along the lines of a developmental unit operating in investment mode. Its staff thus had the opportunity to experiment patiently, assess the still-fluid market, and refine the strategy.

Despite having been launched with the idea of building a corral around research projects that were similar in kind, the now-aggregated projects, each with different parentage, had been competing against each other instead of collaborating. As a first order of business, Adkins conducted a rigorous series of meetings to distill the separate projects into a unified strategy. Doing this successfully required drawing on IBM Box 1 resources beyond the pervasive unit team.

Out of these meetings, the pervasive computing unit adopted the codevelopment process that became a hallmark of IBM's new customer-focused approach to service offerings: in-market testing through partnerships with select customers in areas where the unit saw its richest opportunities. Unlike the mainframe business's legacy focus on the needs of its existing customer base, the unit was competing for new customers whose needs, in many cases, had barely been expressed.

The codevelopment approach was a way of adding to IBM's insight into markets that were still taking shape.

Said Adkins, "Almost everything we did began as an in-market experiment." For example, a team from the pervasive unit worked with a mobile handset provider on a new mobile platform capable of presenting rich data in multimedia formats. The process involved developing a service tailored to the client's unique requirements. "Later, we would harden that into a product that could be replicated for other clients," Adkins continued.

The pervasive unit initially identified four potential platforms for growth: mobile e-business, smart cards, residential gateways (that is, integration of digital home devices, such as TVs, computers, home entertainment systems, and appliances), and telematics (computing inside cars, for example, GPS). However, after conducting in-market experiments, the team decided to focus specifically on mobile e-business and telematics.

All EBOs were required to conduct in-market experiments. The commitment to iterative experimentation is an act of humility; it requires you to admit what you don't yet know. It also is a way to manage down inherent Box 3 risks. The results of the pervasive unit's in-market experiments increased knowledge at a relatively low cost, at the same time helping to harden particular product innovations and service offerings as well as the strategy itself.

This illustrates a key difference between Boxes 1 and 3. In Box 1, you *begin* with strategic clarity (stable markets, familiar customers, time-tested processes), whereas in Box 3, as shown by the EBO experience, your journey allows you to *achieve* strategic clarity through experimentation, assumption testing, and learning.

Many of the technologies the pervasive unit developed in this way—first for individual clients as a test of their potential and later replicated for others—required the expertise of established IBM businesses. So there was a very direct connection between the iterative process of strategy

formation and the ability of a unit leader like Adkins to win the coopera-
tion of his counterparts elsewhere in the company. "At a very early stage,
you learn to manage resources that don't directly report to you," he said.

The resource-allocation process for the pervasive computing unit dif-
fered from the way resources typically were allocated to Box 1 projects.
Rather than funding EBOs based on detailed quantitative justification
or such criteria as internal rate of return and net present value, commitment to an EBO rested on two simple judgments: the idea's attractiveness and the team's track record. Seed capital underwrote many small,
low-cost experiments that explored different directions before the right
path was determined. Funding was released in stages as uncertainties were retired and strategy became clearer. Funds earmarked for
the unit were "ring fenced"—that is, they could not be redirected to
Box 1. The unit's direct line of report to Thompson ensured this. As
Adkins noted, "My funding was relatively protected. This is important.
Otherwise, when things get tough, it is natural to focus on what's tried
and proven—the core businesses. The EBO process allowed us to get
protection around the investments that were needed to pursue the new."

Performance Measurement and Monitoring

A central insight of the EBO process was that IBM suffered from having
only one system of measurement, to which businesses at all stages of
development—emergence, growth, and maturity—had to conform.
The EBO framework incorporated a Box 2 remedy: abandoning traditional short-term financial metrics as the sole basis of evaluation.

An emerging business's performance should be evaluated based
on how well and quickly the team learns from its experiments and
resolves uncertainties. Where senior management of an established
Box 1 business can accurately forecast and easily measure performance by the numbers, a venture like the pervasive computing unit

would best be evaluated by, say, how nimbly its still-evolving strategy could adapt to new information.

When the unit's corporate sponsors (first Thompson and later Harreld) met with Adkins and his senior team, their focus was on how strategy and market development were being sharpened by in-market experiments and other forms of newly acquired insight.

In terms of how to track the unit's progress, Adkins said, "the focus shifted away from purely short-term financial measures." Instead, the EBO management team and its corporate sponsor agreed on project-based milestones. "The milestones were leading indicators of future profits," said Adkins. Among these were such things as the number of agreements for customer pilots and the number of mentions in major media. "John Thompson pushed us on the underlying assumptions behind the strategy and how well we were testing those assumptions," he added.

To sustain momentum, Adkins emphasized the importance of celebrating and publicizing every successfully completed milestone. Teams drew motivation from knowing they were moving in the right direction. The rest of the organization benefited from knowing that something new and of possible relevance to other corners of the enterprise was making progress.

As the unit met more and more milestones, it began to include financial metrics, gradually becoming more rigorous and signaling the approach of a transition from learning to earning. The training wheels eventually were removed and the EBO was ready to "graduate" to the growth stage, eventually to become a successful performance engine.

In a large enterprise like IBM, those transition points are critically important, each marking a change in terms and conditions, said Adkins. "Businesses at different development stages need to be successfully supported with appropriate management and measurement practices. Both *existing* and *emerging* business opportunities serve a purpose at IBM. The world will always be dynamic. What's new today will be 'core' tomorrow, driving the need to find the next big thing."

But managing a portfolio of businesses that "operate under different rules is really very hard to do," Adkins continued. "Box 2 is especially hard in organizations with a long history of success. The EBO structure was a way to overcome the Box 2 challenge. The beauty of the EBO process was that, since it had top leadership support, it allowed us to work through the difficulties and challenges in pursuing new markets, even while maintaining excellence in core businesses . . . Today when you look at it, the EBO philosophy has become part of our culture."

Deep in the weeds of the EBO framework, what IBM devised was a set of activities that together reflect the core Box 2 duty to forget the past—to make unbiased judgments about the day-to-day building of the future without interfering with the important business of the present.

IBM under Ginni Rometty

In 2012, Virginia (Ginni) Rometty succeeded Palmisano as IBM's new chair, president, and CEO, the first woman to occupy those posts. Her first four years have proved challenging. There has been pleasing growth in some new businesses, along with discouraging declines in what once were cash cows but no longer are.

The two-decade transformation overseen by Gerstner and Palmisano didn't focus mainly on divesting lines of business threatened with obsolescence. Instead, it was meant to create a new set of structures, mindsets, and management processes that would protect emerging ventures from disabling Box 1 influence and interference. During her tenure, Rometty has been able to push forward on emerging lines of business while also doing some layoffs and divestitures—including selling IBM's small-server business to China's Lenovo Group Limited and its semi-conductor unit to GlobalFoundries Inc. of Santa Clara, California.

A *Wall Street Journal* article in April 2015 summed up Rometty's challenge this way: "[H]er task is unlike that of past CEOs, who also remade IBM but mainly by shifting toward new markets it could quickly dominate. Ms. Rometty is overseeing a more fundamental shift, turning IBM into a company that also competes where it isn't in a position of strength."[20]

Well, maybe not *yet* a position of strength. Before becoming CEO, Rometty championed IBM's moves into such emergent areas as cloud computing and analytics, markets where IBM could potentially become dominant, but she was also instrumental in revamping the company's legacy mainframe businesses. As I have said before, the Three-Box Solution advocates coexistence, not open warfare, between Box 1 and Box 3. Each serves its purpose, as Adkins and others have noted.

IBM is still in the midst of the same transition that was taking hold when Gerstner arrived. Now, as then, its portfolio consists of a mix of legacy and emerging businesses. Instead of the PCs that threatened Big Blue's mainframe and midrange product lines, cloud computing and truly multiplatform pervasive computing now threaten legacy hardware and software products. At IBM, as in other industries, the shift from revenue models based on "analog dollars" to those based on "digital pennies" is in full swing. And that has had an effect on revenues. As of early 2015, IBM's revenues had declined for twelve straight quarters and its stock price had fallen by 9.6 percent.[21]

A July 2015 article in the *New York Times* latched on to the reality that makes the cannibalization trap so treacherous: "The major trends in technology are often both an opportunity and a threat to IBM. The most notable is the shift to software being delivered from remote data centers as a cloud service, which can curb demand for IBM's traditional software and *undermine its pricing power with corporate customers* [emphasis added]."[22]

Perhaps when judged by those in the Box 1 software business, the transition to a new revenue model might feel like open warfare. But the enterprise is a unified entity, and leaders like Rometty are faced with the responsibility of moving into the future and nurturing new growth. Cannibalization is an unavoidable force, one to be managed rather than denied. As more and more businesses look to the cloud, IBM's customers will demand new software-delivery and payment models.

The *Times* piece noted that second-quarter 2015 cloud-computing revenues were up 70 percent, making it ever more plausible to suppose that technology as a metered utility is finally within reach. Whether change comes fast or slow, it comes inevitably. The wish to allow no cannibalization is a short-term impulse. Rometty appears to be a long-term thinker, forthrightly taking IBM into the future.

In chapter 4, we will look at how the present lays a strong foundation for the future.

Takeaways

- *You must fill Box 2 before you can fill Box 3.* Forgetting precedes learning, and learning requires the humility to concede how much you don't yet know. This is imperative as you begin any Box 3 venture, when uncertainty is at its highest. Therefore, you require a clean slate. Before you can create something new, you have to rid Box 3 of the imprisoning chains of dominant logic. Otherwise, your ability to learn will be severely limited.

- *It is possible to break even the heaviest of chains.* The longer a business has existed and the more impressive its legacy successes, the greater the Box 2 challenge will be of overcoming its dominant logic. Before IBM could reinvent itself as a software and services business for the internet era, it had to divest an increasingly threatened idea: that customers would continue their long devotion to centralized mainframe computing. Box 2 means having the courage to see the many ways in which the past undermines the future.

- **Therefore, the three traps—complacency trap, competency trap, and cannibalization trap—are not irrational anomalies.** They are inevitable, naturally occurring phenomena that have to be understood and attacked head-on. Until they balance the three boxes, organizations will always insist on continuing to invest in the same strategies, skills, and systems that delivered great successes in the past.

- **Box 1 will always fear and hate the prospect of cannibalization. And it won't be mistaken in doing so.** IBM's investments in new strategic lines of business—including big data analytics, cloud computing, and broad integration of mobile platforms—have negatively affected the profitability of some legacy businesses. But that's not a good reason for pulling away from emerging technologies.

- **The first step in formulating a new strategy is to abandon the traditional planning process.** If IBM had allowed its traditional planning regime to remain in place even for emerging businesses, the pervasive computing unit would never have learned that in-market experimentation is an ideal way to achieve strategic clarity in an embryonic market.

- **Box 1 organizations cannot execute nonlinear Box 3 innovation.** Each Box 3 project must follow a zero-based approach defined by its particular vision and specifications. Special teams are essential. To successfully build such teams, use Box 2 as an

active filtration system. Screen out standard organizational practices and preconceptions; replace them with custom-designed
structures and open minds free of dominant logic.

- ***In that spirit, Box 3 must leave behind the strict accountability for results that is so essential in Box 1.*** Instead, allow for
  conjectures about potential nonlinear shifts critical to success in
  Box 3. Those conjectures are best tested by running disciplined
  experiments.

TOOLS

Tool 1: Assess Your Organization's Box 2 Challenge

Selective forgetting begins with identifying aspects of your Box 1 performance engine that threaten development of Box 3 ideas and actions. The critical leadership imperative is to ask, *What policies, structures, training, performance metrics, or other elements in my organization should be forgotten in order to move forward?* The following discussion topics can help your management team overcome the forgetting challenge.

Which of the following statements describe your organization? (Rate each statement on a 5-point scale, where 1 = strongly disagree and 5 = strongly agree.)

- We primarily promote from within.

- We have a homogeneous culture.

- We have a strong culture.

- Our employees have long tenure in the company.

- Other than entry-level positions, we rarely hire from the outside.

- Even when we hire outsiders, we have strong socialization mechanisms.

- We have a long track record of success.

- Our dominant logic is: don't mess with success.

- Our top management team has long tenure in the company.

- Our top management team has worked primarily in the industry in which we compete.

- We rarely recruit from the outside into our top management team.

- We have a strong performance focus that places a premium on meeting short-term financial goals.

If your total score is 36 or above on these 12 statements, your company has a significant "forgetting" challenge to overcome. How will you lead change within this environment?

Tool 2: Identify Your Organization's Box 2 Beliefs

This tool was suggested by Hylke Faber.

Take an honest look at the chains, or orthodoxies—the unchanging truths that cannot be challenged—that dominate decision making in your organization. As in the story of the four monkeys, these "truths" are sometimes invisible and unspoken. Part of creating Three-Box Solutions involves making the chains visible and explicit so you can transform them through disciplined Box 2 actions.

Chains might consist of potentially limiting beliefs about the organization, customers, competitors, regulators, and so on—any and all assumptions that keep dominant logic in place and shut down possibilities for future value creation. As a management team, fill out table 3-1 (add other areas like "technologies").

Tool 3: Target Changes in Your Organization to Facilitate Box 2 and Box 3 Thinking

- Satya Nadella changed the narrative at Microsoft to embrace change and collaboration (discussed in the sidebar). Briefly describe the narrative in your organization. Does it need to change to exploit the power of Box 3? If so, in what ways?

TABLE 3-1

Our Box 2 challenges

Area	Chain/potentially limiting belief system	Potential impact on Box 3 possibilities
Company	"Our company is the best in the world."	Limits scope of external partnering.
		"Not invented here" syndrome.
		Limits learning from weak market signals, e.g., from competitors.
Customers	"Our customers are loyal to us."	Limits focus on new customers.
		Presupposes longevity in relationship where there may not be.
Competitors	"We'll never catch up with the market leader."	Not making bold bets.
		Underestimating the power of internal mavericks.
Regulators	"They will never allow that."	Losing sight of other ways to accomplish the same objective.

Source: this table was suggested by Hylke Faber, founder of Constancee.

- Box 3's success depends on a Box 2 action: forgetting the core definitions and levers of the Box 1 business model. Strategy itself can become orthodoxy when answers to the basic questions that define a business model—Who are our customers? What value do we provide? How do we deliver that value?—become ingrained as second nature. Box 3 must have the freedom to answer these questions differently and even to pursue options that may cannibalize core business revenues. What organizational arrangements—systems, structures, and processes—must you create so that Box 3 can scrub away the dominant logic of the Box 1 business model?

- Box 3 must recognize that a different business model requires different competencies. What changes must you make to your processes of talent acquisition so that Box 3 can break free of the recruitment methods and policies designed to sustain excellence in the core?

- What changes must you make to the performance management system so that Box 3 can forget the Box 1 focus on exploitation of a proven business model and shift to exploration of new possibilities?

- As part of Box 2 actions, identify lines of business that are underperforming or no longer fit the company's strategy (as was the case with TCS's call-center business, discussed in the first sidebar in this chapter). These are candidates for divestiture.

4

Manage the Present

Because most businesses focus almost completely on the Box 1 present, I tend to emphasize disproportionately the work of Boxes 2 and 3 when discussing my framework. Indeed, I see them as the essential tools for creating future business. Yet, the Box 1 performance engine also plays an important role in enabling and supporting Box 3 creation. Consequently, the work of Box 3 becomes all the more difficult in a business where Box 1 is underperforming.

Operating at peak efficiency, Box 1 is the company cash cow. It produces sustaining revenues that are the seedbed for ongoing linear innovations meant to improve the current product mix or optimize the existing business model. Box 1 is also a significant source of funding for Box 3 adventures. Moreover, as we saw in the IBM example, Box 1 can provide either special expertise or market access for conducting the sorts of nonlinear experiments that ultimately develop into future lines of businesses, like those incubated by the pervasive computing unit.

The value of Box 1 cannot be overstated. One executive I work with, Umang Bedi, managing director of Adobe Systems in Bangalore,

India, obsesses about it: "Optimizing Box 1 performance requires setting up operating mechanisms with the key leaders and reviewing key metrics once a week. It also requires spending time with employees to ensure they are truly enabled to deliver their jobs." He clearly understands that he will have no Box 3 without a Box 1 that hums.

So when the Box 1 business suffers reversals or the performance engine fails over time to operate at peak efficiency, repair becomes an urgent matter. In this chapter, I look in depth at how United Rentals, Inc. (URI), the world's largest equipment-rental company, rebuilt its Box 1 business. Its immediate aim was, of course, to improve near-term performance. But CEO Michael J. Kneeland also understood that unlocking long-term growth would be impossible without first fixing Box 1.

The URI example shows how disciplined execution can restore healthy Box 1 performance. It also illustrates some uniquely valuable ways in which Box 2 selective forgetting can be indispensable to the continual reformation and revitalization of Box 1 performance.

In the past, I saw the work of Box 2 as being applied almost entirely to support the Box 3 future. However, good theories need to be flexible in accommodating new evidence. Some of what I learned from the experience of URI has helped me rethink and expand my ideas. I now see the interrelationship of the three boxes as a much more dynamic balancing act. Every business, every day, is always managing, always forgetting, always creating both the linear present and the nonlinear, discontinuous future.

Triple Threats: Box 1 in Crisis

An acquisition deal collapses, a leadership vacuum ensues, and the worst economic shock since the Great Depression decimates the firm's core business. These three circumstances hit URI in swift succession during 2007 and 2008, driving the company's stock price down from nearly $35 a share to just over $3 a share by March 2009. Yet URI's resilient, forceful, and creative strategy over the next several years validated an improbable hypothesis: that the utter failure of a well-conceived acquisition plan can turn out to be a blessing in disguise.

As these events were unfolding, however, Kneeland, then URI's acting CEO, could see only the multiple crises that were knocking the stuffing out of the company's momentum. In due course, Kneeland, along with newly elected board chair Jenne Britell—supported by management and the URI board of directors—would execute an extraordinary Box 1 rebuilding effort that made URI stronger, smarter, and healthier than ever before. Most important, the turnaround left the company better insulated from the buffeting effects of uncontrollable business cycles and better prepared to pursue its Box 3 ideas and opportunities. By 2015, the stock price had climbed to $75 (growth of twenty-five times in market capitalization over a six-year period).

URI ($5.685 billion in 2014 revenues) is the world's largest provider of rental equipment to industrial and construction companies, utilities, municipalities, government agencies, and other organizations.[1] It trades in a diverse array of product categories and (as of early 2015) includes over 430,000 units with an original equipment cost of approximately $8.4 billion. URI's rentable inventory includes earth-moving equipment, aerial lifts, power tools, HVAC systems, pumps, and safety gear.

Founded in 1997, URI grew rapidly, mainly through targeted acquisitions (250 during its first six years) that added customers, geographies, and capabilities. In an industry consisting primarily of many small local players, URI's growth strategy emphasized achieving national scale as quickly as possible.[2] With 1998 revenues of $1.2

billion, it became one of the largest US equipment-rental companies in just its first two years.

By 2007, URI had attracted the attention of private-equity firms as a potential acquisition target. In July of that year, Cerberus Capital Management offered to acquire URI for $34.50 per share. In November, when the deal was about to close, Cerberus abruptly withdrew its offer for unclear reasons. URI sued Cerberus for breach, but in late December, a judge ruled that the private-equity firm was within its rights to walk away as long as it paid a $100 million "breakup" fee, which it did.

The deal's dissolution was a shock. In the summer of 2007, URI was a company fully expecting to be acquired, with the board of directors and management team functioning as caretakers preparing for new ownership. In fact, anticipating the transition, the company's founder and chair, along with the CEO and several board members, stepped down during the sale process. Kneeland was then promoted from chief operating officer (COO) to be the caretaker CEO, tasked with carrying out due diligence related to the acquisition of the company.

Being sold imposes a uniquely short-term focus on a business. The deal itself becomes the strategy, crowding out everything else. Many of the incumbent principals are looking toward futures someplace else, and those who hope to remain can only guess what new ownership will want to do. But by January 2008, all that changed. When Cerberus withdrew its offer, the company's forward momentum suddenly halted. It had no permanent CEO, no board chair, and several board vacancies. In addition to the leadership vacuum at the top, employees across the organization worried about what would come next.

Kneeland, who had spent more than three decades in the equipment-rental industry, had joined URI in 1998. During the following decade, he developed a deep attachment to the company and its people, and he knew he needed to act decisively to change the narrative from the failed acquisition to a tangible scenario for what would come next. There wasn't time to brood about what had gone wrong. "You can't change the past," he said. "You can only change the future."[3]

As URI's former COO, Kneeland was used to being an operations guy, not a strategist. "Nobody asks a COO what he thinks. They just ask him to execute," he said. But he knew the company had two urgent priorities: addressing its leadership vacuum and articulating a new strategic direction. When URI's board began its search for a permanent CEO, Kneeland threw his hat in the ring.

Waves of ominous economic news continued roiling through the first half of 2008. In March, Bear Stearns collapsed and was bought for a relative pittance by JPMorgan, an unthinkable development that spooked the financial sector. Closer to home, the construction industry—URI's largest customer segment—began cooling off. The company couldn't wait for a national CEO search to play out. Whether Kneeland would hand over the company to a new leader or get the job himself, he had to take immediate action. As a first step, he hired Bain & Company to help him formulate a new strategy.

During the period between July 2007 and the end of the year, when the company was under agreement with Cerberus, it was not in a position to appoint new board members or make other significant hires. But after the deal collapsed and the lawsuit ran its course, URI was free to act. The remaining board members began to address the company's leadership vacuum, concluding that URI needed to go in a new direction. In June 2008, the board offered the position of chair to Jenne Britell, the company's newest board member.

Britell had joined the URI board in December 2006, but her first official board meeting was in April 2007, when she and the board learned of the proposal to sell the company to a private-equity firm. From that point on, the focus of board deliberations was on readying the company for sale.

Though Britell was intrigued by the offer to become chair, she still felt like a relative URI novice. There were other people on the board who had more experience with and background at URI. Her initial reaction was to say, "I think you want to get somebody with more history."

On the contrary, she was told, her lack of long history in the company was an asset, not a liability. Britell had spent much of her career in financial services, ending with a position as a senior executive with GE Capital in both domestic and overseas assignments. And she was on a number of other companies' boards. To go in a new direction, the board needed to represent a wider array of perspectives. "You'll look at everything with fresh eyes," one board member told her. Britell accepted the job on the condition that the vote for her candidacy was unanimous.

The Challenge: Restoring Box 1

Although URI had little control over the economic forces that afflicted it, a couple of other circumstances added urgency to its plight. Whenever a company is being acquired, the impending deal introduces distractions that are hard to avoid. URI's preoccupation with the Cerberus deal had diverted some management attention and sown unsettling concerns about the future throughout the company, affecting its ability to deal with a crisis. These concerns were compounded when, after the deal evaporated, the economy worsened throughout 2008, becoming widely catastrophic in 2009. Not only were many of URI's customers concentrated in construction—always vulnerable in a downturn—but another large segment consisted of relatively small, independent local businesses, also likely to suffer early and acutely when the economy sours.

Another part of the problem was structural. The speed with which URI had grown—and attracted the attention of a firm like Cerberus—was beginning to cause problems that further deepened the recession's impact. While URI's strategy of rapid growth by acquisition had been a tremendous success, it now needed to streamline its portfolio of assets. Moreover, so great had been the pace of acquisition that many new properties were left to operate much as they had done previously. This created an eclectic mix of business practices that many customers found confusing or, worse, exasperating.

URI needed to align its various parts around a clearly articulated strategy. It also sought to refocus the way it was organized and managed, and the way it defined its culture and values, more explicitly around customer needs. Finally, the business recognized that it had too many eggs in one or two baskets. It therefore planned to diversify its customer base to become less reliant on vulnerable small businesses and the construction industry as the dominant sources of its business.

Strategy and Opportunity Were Misaligned

Kneeland described URI's original launch strategy as having been built around the goal of achieving growth quickly to get to a critical mass that would enable "power in a multitude—not just for buying equipment, but in just about anything you did that could give you competitive advantage." The strategy also aimed at acquisitions that would build a broad national business rather than concentrated regional strength in dispersed areas (URI is headquartered in Stamford, Connecticut).

Bain's analysis concluded that URI had many solid assets and advantages in place, but its strategy wasn't properly exploiting them. Even though, said Kneeland, the company "had critical mass and a very large footprint, we were primarily going after the small transactional customers who were geographically locked in." Under the original strategy, all customers, small and large, were treated as roughly equal. Consequently, URI was missing out on one of the key advantages of its large accounts' geographical "portability," whereby, through a single point-of-sales contact, URI could have tapped business in multiples states. As it was, all accounts tended to be served at the local level. This meant large customers dealt with an array of local URI offices and were served in uncoordinated, potentially inconsistent ways.

Some Customers Were Both Over- and Underserved

URI's strategy displeased many of its highest-value customers. Bain conducted countless interviews with executives at key URI customer accounts, and Kneeland occasionally went along. "One customer threw down seventeen business cards, most of them from URI," recalled Kneeland, "and then he said, 'Which one's my rep today? Just make it simple. I want one throat to choke!'"

Bain suggested a shift in focus that would manage the distinct needs of three customer tiers: national, regional, and local accounts. Local customers could be dealt with at the level of an individual branch. But in cases where URI's big footprint could produce informational, operational, and economic advantages both for customers and for itself, dedicated sales teams would manage the national and regional accounts.

These sets of larger customers would benefit from scale economies and from coordinated management of their aggregate rental activity and the actionable information it generated. From URI's point of view, these accounts also happened to be better able to manage their way through recessions. National customers in particular could shift resources and activities from region to region in response to more and less favorable economic conditions. And if their business with URI shifted accordingly, the company could rely on established relationships to help it follow the action wherever it went.

Unfortunately, in 2009, URI was neither organized nor motivated in ways that would support such a strategy. It was, in effect, a vast collection of local offices run as fiefdoms and guided by business practices that reflected the preacquisition preferences of much smaller local enterprises. "We had at that time five hundred de facto CEOs and CFOs," said Kneeland. "We needed to shift from territory management to account management. And that was a dramatic change for us."

Fiefdoms Competed for Their Own Benefit

A telling example of the fiefdom mentality is one that Kneeland picked up on during a customer interview. The customer explained that if he needed a piece of equipment—an aerial lift, for example— and it wasn't available from the particular URI office he was dealing with, the office manager wouldn't lift a finger to see if it might be obtained from another URI office on the other side of town. In terms of compensation and incentives, the focus was at the branch level, which naturally reinforced the fiefdoms. If the local office couldn't get credit for the revenue, it said "sorry" to the customer and sent him packing.

There is nothing especially unusual about this type of misalignment. In businesses with growth strategies focused on rapidly reaching a critical mass, full integration of acquired properties is often postponed until some later date—after growth goals have finally been achieved. In Kneeland's estimation, the growth strategy pursued by the predecessor board was, on balance, a great accomplishment. But now the urgent need was to simultaneously take care of loose ends while aligning URI's strategy with its opportunities.

Solutions Began to Take Shape

The bad news was that the company's stock had lost more than 90 percent of its value in a relatively short span of time. The good news, management and the board concluded, was that the fundamentals of URI's growth assets were sound and could be exploited through a combination of strategic clarity and supporting management practices (see table 4-1).

To give key accounts "one throat to choke" and gain for URI the advantage of geographical portability, it was clear to Kneeland that URI should leverage its size and expand its relationships with larger customers. It also needed to diversify its customer base among industrial firms, which would balance out the disproportionate risk of its high percentage of construction accounts.

One of the reasons Kneeland had brought in Bain was that, given his history as an operations guy, he needed to refine his development of company strategy. He was also still in an acting-CEO position while the search for a permanent leader played out. Moreover, URI's board had holdover members, and Kneeland worried about delivering a message that might be misconstrued as a critique of past leadership actions. Although he believed he had a good grasp of the problems the company faced and what needed to be done about them, Bain strengthened his hand with an outside perspective.

TABLE 4-1

Box 1 hallmark principles and activities

Strategy	*Analyze* objective data to achieve strategic clarity.
Execution	*Enact* strategy in a disciplined way, based on clear conclusions.
Support	*Develop* systems and processes to measure, optimize, and sustain execution over time.

Besides Bain, Kneeland also had the benefit of having developed a strong management team, led by CFO Bill Plummer, COO Matt Flannery, and Jeff Fenton. Fenton first worked closely with URI as a partner at Cerberus Capital Management and subsequently joined URI as senior vice president of corporate strategy. During the due-diligence phase of the ill-fated acquisition, Fenton and Kneeland worked together to identify opportunities to achieve improved cost synergies and asset efficiencies. The "playbook" they had created during that process served as a helpful resource in 2008 and 2009.

In late summer 2008, Kneeland presented the final version of the strategy that he and the management team had developed, first to Jenne Britell and later to the board. Britell and the other directors discussed the strategy extensively, approved its recommendations, and offered Kneeland the permanent CEO job.

Turning Around Box 1

Apart from a pressing need in the near term to trim URI's operating costs, Kneeland's strategy amounted to a broad long-range agenda: "We had to change the way we went to market. We had to change the way we thought. We had to change the way in which we measured ourselves. And on top of that, we had to change the way in which we compensated." (See figure 4-1.)

Two Advantages

URI had a couple of advantages as it faced its multiple challenges. First, Cerberus's withdrawal created an urgent crisis a full year before others in the industry began feeling the worst effects of the Great Recession. By the time competitors were scrambling to cut costs, URI

FIGURE 4-1

How URI rebuilt the performance engine

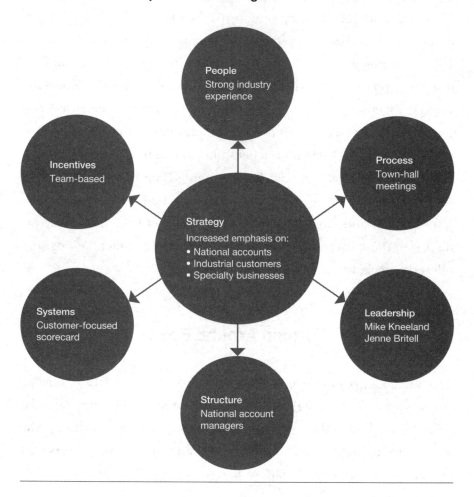

had already done that and moved on to address more long-term strategic concerns. Fenton saw it as a turning point that the company was able to undertake ambitious customer initiatives: "During the hardest of economic times. I think that really helped separate United Rentals from the competition."

URI's cost-control effort was initiated as a component of Kneeland's broader strategy, rolled out as "Operation United" in January 2009.

Often when businesses cut costs, they do it in a blunt, across-the-board way. In achieving its cost efficiencies, URI was much more targeted and strategically minded. The earlier analysis Kneeland and Fenton had done as part of the due-diligence phase of the Cerberus deal helped identify and retain the best-performing branches, including those with the most desirable customer mix (national accounts, a combination of industrial and construction companies). "We pared back about 150 locations," said Kneeland. "We took out about $250 million in permanent cost—$500 million altogether."

A second advantage for URI was the relative immaturity of the equipment-rental sector as a whole. The industry had emerged in the 1960s and '70s as a fragmented slew of local players serving local customers, mainly consisting of small contractors and individual do-it-yourselfers. For a while, it stayed that way. Not until the last decade of the twentieth century did larger competitors emerge. Most of them had grown, like URI, by acquiring local, and sometimes regional, businesses. By the time the Great Recession hit, only a few firms had achieved a truly national footprint, and URI was one of them.

But by the time Operation United kicked off, no one had yet pulled together the management structures, technologies, and processes needed to convert a big footprint into the national-scale economies and compelling customer benefits that would deliver a solid competitive advantage. That was the opportunity Kneeland's strategy envisioned: an ambition to reshape the equipment-rental industry.

Performance Metrics

The consultants Kneeland brought in had accumulated a trove of insights about what customers of all kinds wanted in their relationships with an equipment-rental provider. Among these insights was a short list of key performance indicators (KPIs):

- Providing needed equipment on time

- Providing the equipment from whatever URI branch has it in stock

- Providing quick, responsive service if equipment breaks down

- Providing clear, accurate invoicing promptly

These KPIs were the minimum bar to clear for all customers. But URI's strategy now sought to manage three tiers of customers, each tier with distinct needs. For the larger national and regional clients, there were additional requirements and strategic opportunities. Increasingly, big customers saw equipment rental as a way to lower capital expenditures and convert fixed costs into variable costs.

"Today the market and customers view us as an equipment company," said Fenton, "and that's very true. But we serve another purpose for our customers. We're solving productivity issues. We're solving capital issues. We're helping them manage risk because they don't have to own millions and millions of dollars' worth of equipment. It's not their core competency to buy equipment, to maintain it, to transport it, or to sell it [when it wears out]."

For all those reasons, the percentage of "rental penetration"—the total amount of equipment available from rental firms versus the amount owned by individual businesses—had been rising across the industry over time. Prior to the 1990s, rental penetration was between 5 and 10 percent. From 1990 to 2007, it rose to nearly 40 percent. For URI and its competitors, rental penetration is a fundamental metric of industry health.

In the near term, however, Kneeland was most interested in metrics that would help assess URI's improving health at the branch level.

First, the fiefdom mentality had to be overcome—an application of Box 2 forgetting in the Box 1 arena. To that end, branch managers no longer would be compensated solely on the basis of branch performance; they would also be evaluated on regional performance. To succeed against that goal, branches would have to cooperate rather than compete with each other. Instead of thinking of rental equipment as "belonging to the branch," employees and managers had incentive now to see it as a regionwide pool of assets meant to be freely shared and distributed based on customer needs. (Kneeland established a zero-tolerance policy for any failure to cooperate.)

To be adopted widely, these changed behaviors had to be monitored and measured. The work of developing an up-to-the-minute understanding of URI's performance from the branches on up required an ambitious IT-supported, data-gathering effort. URI rolled out a computerized system to measure every branch against customer-facing business objectives, implementing it down to the branch level and training salespeople and branch managers to use the new tools.

Kneeland wanted to create a culture that was curious about what customers expected and how URI was doing at fulfilling expectations. So the system's goal was to measure every branch's and region's performance on the basic KPIs, which applied to all customers, as well as other indexes that applied to one customer tier or another. For example, how aggressively were regions and individual branches capitalizing on national accounts? If the average branch or region had 20 percent national accounts, why would an outlier have only 5 percent?

The legacy culture of many branch offices—not only at URI, but throughout the equipment-rental industry—was to sit back and wait for business to walk in the door. However, walk-ins are the highest-cost class of customers. This is because of the many touch points required to serve them, the typically small size of their orders, and the low likelihood they will become regular high-volume renters. Conversely, big accounts that do regular business and have established relationships with URI are much less expensive to serve per dollar of revenue. So URI set aggressive thresholds and built in incentives for developing relationships with high-volume renters. These so-called assigned accounts had a single point of contact—one throat—across all the cities, states, and regions in which they operated.

URI's measurement system amounted to a real-time feedback loop and a driver of branch and regional accountability. Sales reps and branch managers were expected to use it. And Kneeland paid particular attention: "I would look at how people were utilizing the system. And I would go to IT and say, 'Look, I need to know activity: Who's signing in? Who's not signing in?' Because that tells me when someone is just giving me the nod and saying he's doing it [when he's not]."

In Kneeland's view, if URI could achieve a more unified, well-coordinated, and tightly disciplined approach to serving its three customer segments, the market would reward its improved performance. In the long run, if URI succeeded in reshaping the business, rental penetration would rise higher; 65 or 70 percent was not unthinkable.

Adding Bench Strength

Just as Britell would use director vacancies to bolster the URI board's expertise in certain areas (see later), Kneeland pursued similar opportunities to strengthen his management team, starting in 2009. Recall that when Keurig (chapter 2) needed to enhance its Box 3 innovation capabilities, Kevin Sullivan, the chief technology officer, steered clear of kitchen-appliance expertise. Instead, he sought people from outside the industry, such as aeronautical engineers. His goal was to drive nonlinear thinking. In Box 1, Kneeland's objective was different: to enrich URI's overall experience within certain areas of the linear frame. In sales and marketing, strategy, and business development, he added a handful of senior executives who together brought 140 years of experience in equipment rental.

These reinforcements (Fenton among them) fit well with URI's focus on its core business: the reformation of branch culture and behavior, the three-tiered marketing strategy, and the optimization of a range of foundational business processes. Furthermore, in the still-evolving equipment-rental space, there were opportunities to execute a number of linear innovations.

Turning Metrics into Information Products

URI's strategy also envisioned that an enhanced ability to capture performance data would enable it in the long term to add new kinds of value for its most profitable national and regional customers. Giving them one throat to choke was tactically important. But what if URI could also help them manage their overall rental activities more efficiently and cost effectively and, for instance, with a higher awareness of user safety? That would be strategic. And it was the next logical step after having developed the IT systems and processes for measuring URI's own performance. As their by-product, those initiatives would also capture utilization data, which ultimately could be converted into actionable insight—strategic, logistic, economic, and operational—that customers would pay to obtain.

Sometimes the borderline between Boxes 1 and 3 is unclear. The key distinction between linear Box 1 innovation and nonlinear Box 3 innovation is that Box 3 requires a discontinuous leap to a new business model with the power to transform industry competition. In a celebrated example, American Airlines used emerging technology in the 1970s to power Sabre, its legendary computerized reservation system. Sabre was intended as a Box 1 performance booster that could give American a competitive advantage over other airlines. But the reservation system soon evolved into a very profitable Box 3 business in its own right.

For the longer term, said Fenton, URI saw similar potential to shape utilization and performance data into value-adding products: "We'd like to kind of transform ourselves into a solutions-based company. We're never going to exit the equipment component, but there's much more that we can bring to the table if customers start to view us and value us that way because we need to get paid for something beyond supplying equipment." That extra something could be insight and expertise.

Building an Energized Board of Directors

The revitalization of URI's board of directors played a key role in turning the company around. It is easy to underestimate the contributions an active, well-functioning board can make. Even many reasonably diligent boards are not especially hands-on. But as URI's new chair, Britell wanted the directors to engage as energetically as possible with URI's challenges as a way of giving new CEO Kneeland their full support. So she encouraged a high level of engagement.

For example, early in Britell's tenure, the company needed to fill three board vacancies. Before retaining an outside search firm, she and Kneeland discussed what expertise gaps on the existing board could be filled by new directors. They concluded that URI would benefit from deeper expertise in three areas: IT, logistics, and sales and marketing. IT would power URI's ability to monitor and analyze its real-time performance. Logistics expertise would help improve URI's numerous asset management processes while also helping it develop the high-level insights that would populate the information products it aspired to offer its best customers. And deep sales and marketing experience would help URI tailor offerings to its three tiers of existing customers as well as broaden its appeal among the industrial accounts it needed in greater numbers. To validate their conclusions, Britell asked current board members for their views on the "missing" capabilities. Their consensus matched Kneeland and Britell's earlier conclusions. These perspectives were shared with the search firm, and the search for the three vacancies proceeded.

Britell then invited every incumbent board member to read the search firm's briefing book and analysis of potential candidates and to individually interview each one—multiple times, if they thought it useful. All of them did so. Although that level of participation was unusual (candidate vetting typically was delegated to a small subset of directors) and accommodating it created a longer process, Britell saw it as a worthwhile investment. She believed it would help avoid situations "where the board was divided on critical issues or felt they were not included."

As a result, even before any of the newly hired directors attended their first board meeting, all had become well acquainted with the other directors' views of the company, the issues URI faced, and its culture. And all were socially comfortable interacting as peers with incumbent board members. Moreover, the process began to build a habit of engagement that spread to other areas.

For example, Britell and Kneeland strongly urged board members to visit local URI branches while traveling on business. Some directors made arrangements through Kneeland to schedule formal visits, but others sometimes simply dropped by a local branch when they had some spare time. Through these and other activities, URI's directors developed a nuanced understanding of the company and its people. Kneeland was so pleased with the way the board was evolving that he invited Britell and the other directors to attend his annual management meetings. He also asked Britell to moderate board roundtables at meetings that included branch and district management teams, who were invited to submit questions. These board-member panels were often among the sessions rated highest by attendees, one of whom, said Britell, wrote, "It makes me feel better to know we have a board that really knows what they're doing."

Finally, board members, Kneeland, and other company leaders participated in numerous town hall–style meetings with local-branch employees (see the sidebar, "How to Engage the Rank and File"). Many of these meetings were held in the wake of URI's merger with RSC Holdings (more on this later)—the company's main national-scale rival—to get a clearer sense of how well the firms were meshing.

Growing the Base of Industrial Customers

URI's disproportionate reliance on customers in the construction sector continued to be a challenge. For that reason, it proved fortuitous that Jenne Britell would occasionally meet with Denis Nayden, a managing partner at Oak Hill Capital Partners. Oak Hill was one of the main investors in RSC and Nayden served as its board chair. RSC had a high percentage of the kinds of industrial customers URI coveted. Britell and Nayden, who became acquainted when they both worked at GE Capital, would meet over a period of a few years to talk about a possible transaction, but the idea never moved past the stage of informal conversations, said Britell.

Nonetheless, the fact that they kept talking made sense. A combination of the two firms would create the world's largest player in the equipment-rental industry. Perhaps more important for URI, the instant infusion of RSC's industrial customers would help URI hedge its disproportionate vulnerability to economic shocks affecting the construction sector.

"And then," recalled Britell, "in November of 2011, I called Denis and I said, 'You know, we don't really want to be sitting in a retirement home someday, saying, "There was that one missed deal . . . and why couldn't we make it work?'" So we met for dinner right before Thanksgiving, and I said, 'Denis, the board told me to get things going, OK?'"

Britell said the RSC deal took shape within two weeks after that dinner: "It was an extraordinary transaction. And when it closed in 2012, Mike and his team did an extraordinary job of leading the integration—and particularly Matt Flannery, our COO. It was as good an integration as I've seen done anywhere."

Often, the defining quality of a successful integration is that the acquiring party—in this case, URI—resists the temptation to behave heavy-handedly when making key personnel decisions. Said Kneeland, "Failure comes about in transactions because they don't keep the [right] people. So we made a very strong statement that this is going to be done on the basis of 'the best available athlete.' And it started at the senior level. There were hard choices to make, and when we started making them, that cascaded down."

Kneeland demanded a very tough level of justification for any recommendation to select a legacy URI person over someone from RSC: "We did it together—collectively, their team and our team—on everything. For every line item, whether it was technology, sales, accounting, you name it, we had equal amounts of representation on both sides."

The result was a peaceful, positive, rancor-free transition to a well-integrated company with the power to outperform competitors. The combined company was not just larger, it was also better. RSC not only added a significant number of industrial accounts that URI lacked, but also brought the distinct skills and expertise required to service industrial customers. On every level, including the addition of three experienced directors from RSC, the merger made Box 1 sense.

How to Engage the Rank and File

Turning around a business is an all-hands endeavor. Not just at the top of the pyramid, but at every level of the organization. Mike Kneeland's many years in the equipment-rental industry had led him to value highly the role of rank-and-file employees in generating and sustaining customer satisfaction and loyalty.

"We're a service organization, and I've always believed that what stands between us and the customer is our people. And if you can't engage with people, then you should be in some other sort of industry," Kneeland said. But the company had been through a series of bruising changes, and its people needed some attention. Kneeland embarked on an ambitious companywide communications effort that included town hall–style meetings in all of the cities where URI had branches. For him and the other executives who presided, each of these meetings (many of which were attended by board members) was actually an all-day event, culminating in an evening briefing for hourly employees and other staff from the area branches. Here is Kneeland's self-described approach to these meetings:

> I can't tell you how many town halls I did. Every other week I was at a town-hall meeting in one of our major metropolitan areas. Say I'm in Boston, where we've got six branches . . . During the day, I would go to

Adding Specialty Goods to General Rental Equipment

URI had identified one further opportunity to optimize its Box 1 performance. Most of the larger firms in the equipment-rental sector dealt mainly in "general rental" items—the diverse array of tools and equipment their customers used daily for common work activities. Prior to the recession, general-rental products constituted nearly the entire inventory of URI's offerings. URI and other general-rental firms had left to a class of niche providers a second *all six branches and talk to the hourly employees. And then I'd have lunch with the management and sales teams and I'd share with them what I heard. After that, I would stop and listen to them. We learned how to listen better—how to listen to what we needed to hear and not just what we wanted to hear.*

Then, at 5:00, I would meet and greet the hourly employees only—no management, just hourly employees and me—from 5:00 to 6:00. Then the rest of the staff would arrive and we would have dinner. After dinner, I would talk to them about who we are, where we are now, where we intend to go, and how they're important to those plans.

I also wanted to know from them on certain topics—customer safety, customer service, employee relations—how we could become better. They would break up into four groups and try to figure out what was going wrong. But I always said, "Don't just treat it as a gripe session. Tell me what's not working, but also tell me what has to be true in order to make it better." After that, all four groups had to present to everybody.

I was always very happy with what we did in those meetings. After our off-site last year, we commissioned an independent employee-engagement survey. We had the highest scores ever in terms of engagement with employees.

rental category consisting of "specialty" goods, those with utility for specialized tasks and projects that lay outside most customers' normal daily activities. For example, a single specialty renter might focus only on the kind of equipment required for safely digging trenches (such as systems of steel reinforcing walls that guard against trench collapse). Another might focus on providing large electric generators used to power construction sites, movie locations, event venues, and so forth. Yet another might rent industrial pumps and related paraphernalia.

URI had not previously considered an extensive build-out of the specialty field. Indeed, the divide between general and specialty rental firms had been embedded into the way the industry was organized. Among the reasons for this, said Fenton, was that specialty equipment often "requires unique sets of skills to sell it, rent it, and maintain it." Just thinking about making the leap called for some Box 2 forgetting.

It helped that there were a number of compelling factors that favored entering the specialty market. First, especially with the addition of RSC, many of URI's existing large customers had a recurring need for specialty equipment. Second, the profit margin on specialty items was significantly higher than that for general items. Third, URI's broad customer base gave it added buying power to compete effectively with a range of specialty providers and possibly even to acquire some.

By 2015, URI rented a range of specialty equipment, including large electric generators, HVAC systems, trenching systems, and industrial pumps of the kind used in oil and gas drilling. Fenton noted that during Hurricane Sandy in 2012, temporary URI HVAC and power systems were deployed in New York City high-rise buildings.

These aren't the sorts of items you can walk in and rent from a typical URI branch. Specialty equipment tends to be complicated and requires special expertise to transport, operate, and maintain. That explains why URI had invested $800 million to acquire a pump-rental firm in 2014. "Obviously, it's a very large investment," said Fenton. "Pumps are a specialty product. Many of them go to oil and gas fields across North America. You have to provide a level of engineering. You provide many other things than just the pump. You set it up on-site. You maintain it. It's there for a long period of time. And what it does is a very, very critical function. If the pump stops working, it usually shuts down the job site."

Knocking down the traditional wall between rental categories certainly helped further Kneeland's expectation that URI could reshape the equipment-rental industry.

Looking to the Future

By 2012, Box 1 had significantly rebounded. URI had become aggressively customer focused. It had aligned the branches and regions—and sales teams—with its three-tiered marketing strategy. It had diversified its customer base with the goal of making itself less vulnerable to volatile economic swings. With the entry into specialty rentals, URI offered customers a wider range of products and services. And the high-margin specialty business allowed revenues to grow at a faster clip.

"We will still have cycles," said Kneeland, "but we think they will be less dramatic because of our diversification."

Turning to the Box 3 future, Kneeland challenged Fenton to develop strategies that would actually allow URI to continue growing through a downturn. "I don't know exactly what that looks like," he said, "but I've told him not to let equipment be the only thing on his mind." Kneeland pledged to provide enough funding so that Fenton could explore and experiment in whatever directions looked promising. In a sense, Fenton's task became figuring out what URI's future core competencies will be.

URI also possesses a data warehouse stocked with more than fifteen years of transactional and utilization data that can be groomed over time into a variety of information products that help customers consume rental services more intelligently and economically. "There are jewels in that data," said Kneeland. Interestingly, he put Bill Plummer, URI's CFO (whom Kneeland describes as a "very brilliant" MIT-trained aeronautical engineer who is "not from the accounting world"), in charge of finding those jewels. "I've got to believe there are opportunities we haven't uncovered yet."

And he told Dale Asplund, his CIO, "I want to digitize the company." Although he was unsure what it would take to do that, the broad idea was to make it possible for many more customer interactions to be accomplished digitally.

Kneeland has been canny in delegating these areas of future exploration to a handful of different executives. Putting them all on one person's shoulders felt wrong, he said. "I didn't want it to get clogged up." Moreover, he said, "They each have their own sets of attributes that are good and forward thinking. So I wanted them to look at the world differently and separately."

By 2015, while Box 1 was healthy, the leadership never considered the "mission accomplished." Toward that end, Kneeland had targeted continuous improvement as a desirable core competency. He had brought new talent to URI with expertise in *kaizen*, lean thinking, and other process-improvement disciplines. He required all management to spend at least one week a year in kaizen training. He described a kaizen session he went through himself with a mechanic, a truck driver, a branch manager, and a district manager. They were trying to reduce the time it took—wheels in to wheels out—to load an equipment delivery truck. The starting point was a process that had timed out at between thirty-five and fifty-five minutes. "By the end of the week, we had mapped out a process and had it implemented. We got it down to fifteen minutes and we did it collectively. I thought that was enormously powerful," Kneeland said.

While Kneeland and others had the confidence to turn increasingly to nonlinear Box 3 thinking, the company had absorbed the lesson that all three boxes require regular attention—that nothing can ever be taken for granted.

"I believe that I can always learn something and apply it," said Kneeland. "That's how I think. That's how I operate."

In chapters 5 and 6, we will look more closely at the challenging art of balancing the amount of attention invested in all three boxes.

Takeaways

- *Box 1 excellence begins with strategic clarity, executed with discipline and supported by systems and processes that sustain a high level of performance.* At URI, a variety of circumstances converged to cause a lack of full clarity and strategic alignment. Any business that finds itself in that position needs to step back and reconnect with its core: its customers, mission, employees, and culture. Areas of performance that have gone awry may benefit from a dose of Box 2 forgetting.

- *Healthy Box 1 performance is essential to Box 3 creation.* For Box 3 ideas to be relevant, the business must live to fight another day. Box 1 first and foremost funds the present. To do more than that, it must not only be stable but also prosperous enough to build value that can be invested in the future. URI methodically rebuilt its performance engine to the point where it could meet both challenges.

- *A fully engaged board of directors is invaluable to an organization's resiliency.* Many of Board Chair Jenne Britell's efforts to involve the board in key decisions were undertaken to support new CEO Kneeland's strategy. But they also substantially strengthened the organization in numerous interrelated ways. And Kneeland actively welcomed directors to attend company meetings and visit URI branches whenever they liked. The productive partnership between Kneeland and Britell is an example worth emulating.

- *Optimizing current business models in Box 1 requires different activities, skills, methods, metrics, mind-sets, and leadership approaches than those used to create new business models in Box 3, but both boxes must be pursued simultaneously.* Moreover, there is a symbiotic relationship between Box 1 and Box 3 that is of optimal value only when Box 1 is functioning properly.

- *The key distinction between linear Box 1 innovation and nonlinear Box 3 innovation is that Box 3 requires a discontinuous leap to a new business model with the power to transform industry competition.* As URI regained its stride, there were two key transitional moves that made industry transformation a more tangible objective: the acquisition of RSC and the unconventional move to add specialty rental assets to URI's equipment inventory. These were classic examples of planned opportunism—preparing for the future before it arrives.

- *A leader's capacity to understand the human dimensions of difficult business decisions can drive a healthy transparency.* Kneeland, Britell, and others in the URI leadership ranks recognized that they needed to be visible and forthright during the process of restoring Box 1 performance and implementing changes for the future. Their openness in answering employees' questions in town-hall meetings and other forums enhanced understanding across the company of why moves were being made and what the stakes were.

TOOLS

Tool 1: Assess the Health of Your Box 1

As a management team, focus on your Box 1 performance engine and answer the following questions:

- Do you have a solid understanding of your industry's structure in terms of the bargaining power of suppliers and customers, the intensity of direct rivalries, entry barriers, and the threat of substitutes?

- What is the competitive advantage of your business model and product offerings? Why will customers prefer your products or services over those your competitors offer?

- Describe your organization in terms of formal reporting structure, decision authority, information flows, and task-and-process flows that shape decision making. Does your formal organization suit the requirements for sustaining your business's competitive advantage?

- Describe the ways your company motivates and measures against performance goals (that is, compensation and incentive systems). Do those systems successfully support the execution of the performance engine strategy?

- Describe your resource-allocation and planning processes. Do they successfully support achieving and sustaining your competitive advantage?

- Describe your human resources (HR) approach in terms of selecting, training, developing, evaluating, promoting, and firing employees and building competencies. Is your HR approach well aligned with the goal of building your competitive advantage?

- Describe your culture in terms of valued behaviors and common beliefs and norms that implicitly or explicitly guide managerial actions. Does your culture support execution of Box 1 strategy?

Tool 2: Strengthen Your Box 1

- Describe the key initiatives that during the next twelve months will help you eliminate performance gaps that exist in Box 1.

- Have you allocated sufficient resources to execute these key initiatives?

- Have you assigned individuals to lead these initiatives and established appropriate accountability metrics for their performance?

5

Keeping the Three Boxes in Balance

The Three-Box Solution requires an ability to think and act simultaneously in multiple time frames. As we've seen in the examples throughout this book, you're always managing the present, destroying the past, and building the future. At times, you will have to focus more on one box than the others, but the tools in this book will help you attend to all three boxes with your teams and others in your organization.

But what happens when things get truly out of balance? How do you keep all three boxes going at once?

To address this question, we look to the unlikely story of Willow Creek Community Church—an organization run by MBAs and that is the subject of a popular Harvard Business School case—to see how an organization can keep the three boxes in perfect balance over time.

Reinventing Church

The Willow Creek Community Church, and later the Willow Creek Association, grew out of an uncommonly sharp observation by a 1960s middle-school student named Bill Hybels. Hybels was aware that the suburban Midwest Protestant church his family attended supported the work of missionaries who were "trying to help people find faith in Jesus Christ" in Africa, Asia, and other faraway places. That "made perfect sense from a mission standpoint, as long as it happened overseas," said Hybels. "But it seemed a bit odd to me that there were no similar kinds of conversations happening in our church leadership about people without faith who lived a few blocks away." Hybels even recalled telling his father that the best way for a nonreligious local family to find faith would be to travel to Africa, "where one of our missionaries could have a conversation with them."

Although he didn't forget about his insight, the teenage Hybels was in no position at the time to tackle the problem. And, in any case, his life was following a different trajectory. His father ran a number of businesses, including a prosperous and growing wholesale produce company. "The whole script of my life was to follow in my father's footsteps and run his companies," Hybels commented. So Hybels went off to college and studied business and economics. He continued, "There was really no thought to it. I loved working in this company; I'd done so since junior high age. Nothing else had any appeal to me because I understood the business."

However, during his college years, Hybels experienced an instance of near-seismic religious awakening. He describes it as a "direct, personal encounter with the living God." It produced in him a feeling so transforming that "all of a sudden, the selling of fruits and vegetables . . . paled in comparison with the challenge of helping everyday people discover the immensity of the love of God." In what he recalled was "a difficult conversation," he told his father he had had a change of heart.

As Hybels discussed religion with a group of like-minded friends, together they began to hatch plans to start a church. It would not be the sort of traditional church his family had belonged to in his youth, but one that would "try to make the message of Christianity understandable to people with no faith or damaged faith."

The 1960s and '70s were an era of rapidly declining church attendance. Hybels had an instinct about the causes of growing secularization: the world was changing in dramatic ways, but churches were failing to change with it. There was nothing wrong with the substance of the Protestant message, but the style in which it was delivered was antiquated. Worse, when many of those without faith were exposed to traditional churches, they often felt judged for their faithlessness and heavily pressured to embrace religion.

In 1975, drawing on his business education, Hybels conducted market research to test the validity of his instincts.[1] He and his compatriots surveyed thousands of "unchurched" people to see why they did not attend or belong to a church. The responses boiled down to a handful of reasons: Churches were "always asking for money." Services were described as "boring and lifeless" or "predictable." Sermons lacked "real world" relevance. Those who attended would go home feeling worse than when they arrived because "the pastor made [them] feel guilty and ignorant."

Out of those frank insights, Hybels and the other founders conceived a new kind of church built around a refreshingly modern service. They would use contemporary music, drama, dance, and video—whatever it took to connect with modern people. And where the church that Hybels grew up in had thought of the irreligious "in almost hostile terms," Willow Creek Community Church would welcome skeptics with open arms and treat them with respect. The church would not ask newcomers for money. There would be no hard selling, no pressure tactics. People would want to join because the foundational Protestant message was delivered in an authentic and engaging way and because the church was a comfortable place in which to receive it.

Balancing the Three Boxes

In this chapter and the one that follows, we'll explore from different perspectives the challenge of achieving balance among the three boxes. This chapter considers balance a matter of operational discipline and process, whereas chapter 6 looks at balance as the product of six categories of leadership and organizational behavior. Both perspectives are essential to the Three-Box Solution.

Balance necessarily begins at the top with a leader who understands that the boxes interrelate. Willow Creek has been fortunate to have two leaders—Bill Hybels, later joined by Jim Mellado—who saw clearly that *preservation*, *destruction*, and *creation* are part of a cyclical process of renewal. Hybels speaks of this cycle in the context of the well-known verses of Ecclesiastes 3: "To every thing there is a season, and a time to every purpose under heaven: A time to be born, and a time to die; A time to plant, and a time to pluck up that which is planted; A time to kill, and a time to heal; A time to break down, and a time to build up."

In a very real way, balance requires you to attend daily to each of the seasons and purposes. To be able to make that commitment of daily attention, there is perhaps nothing more useful than the various preparedness measures I described in earlier chapters as *planned opportunism*—all of the initiatives spanning all three boxes that act as a hedge against the unpredictability of the future.

For example, you can empower individuals and formal teams, as Hasbro's Brian Goldner and United Rentals' Mike Kneeland have done, to prospect for weak signals, Box 3 ideas, and new operating strategies. You can develop tailored management styles and metrics for businesses at different stages of development, as IBM's EBO process specified. And as we will see in chapter 6, you can encourage and protect the idiosyncratic mavericks in your midst—people with important ideas and insights but low levels of influence or political skills.

The key to understanding balance is to recognize the linkage among the three boxes. As we learned in chapter 4, Box 3 would be disadvantaged without a prosperous and strategically aligned Box 1. And without a well-functioning Box 2, dominant logic, structures, and practices of Box 1 would make Box 3 ventures impossible. Box 2 serves as a cleansing mechanism that wipes away barriers imposed by the past. Those barriers typically are hardwired in the values and practices required by the Box 1 business, which cannot function effectively without them. But they have to be forgotten in Box 3 so that creation can occur in a "clean slate" condition, uncluttered by past ideas or practices.

The Willow Creek Community Church—named for the old Willow Creek Theatre in Palatine, Illinois, where services originally were held—was born out of an abundance of weak signals and Box 2 insights. The church was explicitly designed in reaction to what its founders believed were the obsolete trappings and self-defeating priorities of traditional churches. In essence, Willow Creek would serve as an answer to the powerful objections that were driving away so many people from churches of every denomination.

Those founding motives may well have embedded Box 2 thinking in the fabric of Willow Creek. That certainly appears to be the case, for in the forty years since its founding, the organization repeatedly has renewed itself by letting go of old activities and practices, sometimes even before they showed obvious signs of being past their prime. As you will see later, at Willow Creek, this Box 2 practice is a formal, regularly occurring part of the management process.

Indeed, such diligence cannot be left to chance. As I have stressed all along, Box 2 is the biggest challenge for most businesses. I believe it is harder for an organization to admit to itself that *it's time to stop doing something* than to know when *it's time to invent something new.* Though these two thoughts inevitably go hand in hand, ceasing an established activity can be like losing an old friend. There are powerful emotional attachments that must be overcome. And frequently there are wrenching human consequences involved in letting go. But a capacity for renewal is the foundation of organizational sustainability. A discipline consisting of unsentimental Box 2 practices and processes is required in order to enable a pattern of cyclical renewal—the most compelling benefit of the Three-Box Solution.

In the quest for balance, a need for process applies in all three boxes. As Hybels put it, "Church is an organization, just like GE. We need to create formal operating mechanisms, just like a business organization, to keep the three boxes in balance."

A pastor can find the idea of creating operating mechanisms of any kind difficult to embrace. "Most pastors go to seminary, learn Greek and Hebrew, and learn how to exegete passages from the Bible, which is all extremely important stuff," said Hybels. But after they've preached their first Sunday sermon, "they get up on Monday morning and realize they're the CEO of an organization that has employees, that has a payroll, that has an HR function, that has land to acquire, strategic plans to put together, and boards to work with. And they have had none of that preparation."

Hybels, however, did have that preparation. In addition to his business major and economics minor, he had grown up with a business-minded father and had spent his spare time working in the family business. Business thinking came naturally. He put it to use creating a church designed to deliver a new kind of religious experience for the faithful and, most importantly, to attract and convert to faith the growing legions of the unchurched.

In this chapter, I draw mainly on Willow Creek and secondarily on Tata Consultancy Services, India's largest technology business, to show how organizations can continue to execute dramatic changes over the decades by balancing the three boxes. In both examples, you will see how processes and operating disciplines helped very different entities make the most of the present, face up to the depleted assets of the past, and remain alert to the opportunities of the future. You will see too that balancing the three boxes is a continuous process rather than a set of occasional events, making it imperative to think of balance as a form of systemic discipline.

I'll look at three of Willow Creek's cyclical innovations, beginning with the church's founding moves to reinvent worship services for a modern flock.

First Box 3 Innovation: Worship plus Outreach

Hybels approached inventing the church in a process-rich, systematic way. He saw church as serving four foundational purposes: *exaltation* (gathering members together to glorify God through worship), *edification* (helping believers deepen their spiritual life through participation in the church), *evangelism* (reaching out to "unchurched Harry and Mary," who were also referred to as "seekers"), and *social action* (becoming "a conscience to the world" by embodying God's love "in word and deed").[2]

In 1975, the Willow Creek Community Church had two main goals: to reinvent the antiquated model of the worship service so that it would feel contemporary and relevant to modern parishioners, and to construct a system of outreach to the unchurched that would be welcoming and nonjudgmental, designed to proceed at a pace set by the seeker, not the church.

Reinventing the Service

Several components contributed to the goal of reinvigorating and contemporizing the service of worship:

- *Music.* Gone were the traditional pipe organ and the eighteenth- and nineteenth-century hymns. Instead, there was a live band playing modern instruments.

- *Drama.* The pastor distilled lessons from the Bible into parables conveyed through contemporary predicaments that better connected the scripture to churchgoers' daily lives. Within each service, these dramas looked ahead to the message of the sermon.

- *Multimedia.* The service often combined music with video and photography, making for more-immersive sensory experiences.

- *Putting scripture in a modern context.* Like the drama segments, readings from scripture were explicitly linked to current events or predicaments and prefigured the theme of the sermon.

In the 1970s, the trend of growing secularization left no denomination untouched. Churches within a given faith competed with each other over a dwindling supply of church members. Growth in one church thus came at the expense of others. Willow Creek understood that this was a zero-sum game. The best way to grow organically was to increase the supply of believers by appealing to the unchurched, a group that was likely to include many disenchanted former church members. Beginning with its revamped worship service, Willow Creek was designed to do just that.

System of Outreach

In order to turn such people into faithful Christians, the church developed a detailed methodology. From its roots, Willow Creek was rich in process and valued the benefits of disciplined operational practices. The process of reaching out to seekers, bringing them into the fold, deepening their faith, and then equipping them to reach out to other unchurched individuals was spelled out in a "7-Step Strategy," with each step explained in considerable detail and supported by underlying reasoning (see figure 5-1).

The strategy began with encouraging believers to develop "relationships of integrity" with the unchurched.[3] Integrity meant that believers needed to be open and honest with seekers about their faith and to tell their own stories in a compelling way. (Willow Creek also developed a four-week training program to help church members understand the needs of seekers and communicate with them effectively.)[4]

Another core principle of outreach was that believers and seekers were different enough that they required separate worship services, tailored to their respective needs. Seekers needed to discover—or rediscover—faith, whereas believers needed to deepen their understanding of it. Seeker services were offered at convenient times on Sunday, whereas members and believers attended services on weekday evenings. This inverted the logic that dominated traditional churches, which typically catered to members over nonmembers (or, in business terms, existing over prospective customers). But Willow Creek, acting on Hybels's teenage insight, had repatriated the missionary spirit, making it the church's main work to reach those who had drifted away from faith.

FIGURE 5-1

Willow Creek Community Church seven-step strategy for reaching "unchurched Harry/Marry"

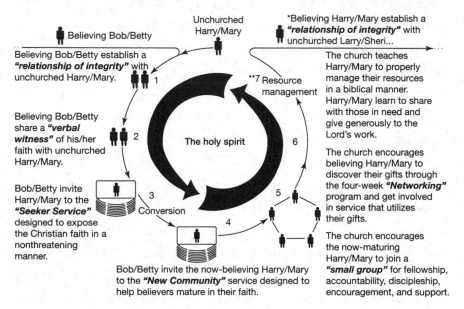

*Start of new cycle can actually begin right after conversion.
**Over 95 percent of staff were from people reaching this step within the church.
Source: Leonard A. Schlesinger and Jim Mellada, "Willow Creek Community Church (A)," 691-102 (Boston: Harvard Business School Publishing, 1991).

Likewise, during the offering portion of a seeker service, the unchurched were explicitly asked not to contribute to the collection plate. Put simply, the church treated seekers to a free trial that would last as long as it took either to bring them to faith or to lead them to conclude that Willow Creek was not for them. Therefore, at the end of each seeker service, Hybels would deliver a respectful, deliberately low-pressure message that went something like this: "We believe you're intelligent people . . . with adequate brain power and self-reflection capabilities. What you do with what we just presented to you is between you and God, or you and your family. If you decide you'd like to learn more, hop on for the ride. If you decide you're not interested right now, we are not offended; go live your life! If you change your mind and we can help later on, we'll be here."

Creating the Best Possible First Impression

As with almost any example of a well-executed strategy, the Willow Creek approach featured extraordinary attention to detail from the very beginning. Church leaders thought hard about the impression Willow Creek would make on first-time visitors. They envisioned the path seekers would take upon arriving at the church, calling it "Main Street" and designing every aspect of the church to create as pleasing an impression as possible—from the well-tended grounds to a staff of attentive volunteers on hand to funnel visitors to parking places, help them make their way into the church, and answer any questions they might have (though in a low-key rather than overwhelming way).[5] The attention to detail could be remarkably fastidious. According to the head of building maintenance, "We don't even like using any 'out of order' signs anywhere in the building because we see that as sending a message that 'it has been broken for some time.'"[6]

Whereas some churches routinely ask newcomers to stand during services and make themselves known to the regular members, Willow Creek had learned through its research that seekers—at least, at the start—value their anonymity and prefer not to be singled out. So there would be no adhesive badges saying, "Hi, my name is . . . " In any case, most seekers first attended a Willow Creek service at the invitation of members who had established a relationship with them. The respectful acknowledgment of seekers' preferences was part of the larger belief that their journey to joining the faith would depend on accepting the church's authentic, compelling message and spirit, about which they would make up their minds, one way or the other, without being pressured.

Over time, the low-pressure method proved amazingly successful. Hybels said the very first service at the Willow Creek Community Church attracted about 125 worshipers. "That dwindled down to about 60 before it stabilized and then started to grow. These days, we would have about 27,000 people attend on a regular weekend."

As it has grown, Willow Creek keeps focus on continuous innovation. For example, in 2014, the Willow Creek Community Church embarked on an experiment, called "The Practice," to consider new ways of delivering Christian learning and converting it into daily action. In an interview with *Leadership Journal*, a publication of Christianity Today, Willow Creek pastors Steve Carter and Aaron Niequist described some of the work of their eighteen-month experiment.

"We talk a lot about a gymnasium metaphor," said Niequist. "Teaching is important for growth, but sitting in a classroom can only take you so far. When we look at what we do in most church gatherings, it's centered on a lecturer. It's a classroom. But if I want to learn how to run a marathon, I wouldn't want to go hear a lecture about a marathon. I'd want to train with a coach. And so we asked, 'What if a church was more like a gymnasium than a classroom? What if the church gathering was a time when we came together to practice rather than just listen?' It's a different kind of learning. That's why we're calling our experiment 'The Practice.' The focus is on the disciplines of the Christian life and the different practices that train us to go out and practice what Jesus said Monday through Saturday."[7]

Carter talked about what it takes for Box 1 and Box 3 to sustain a positive relationship: "I think at the core there must be trust. Box 1 has got to trust that Box 3 is not trying to destroy or replace it. At the same time, Box 3 has got to be gracious and thankful to Box 1 for providing the opportunity to do its experimentation. All of that requires leaders in both boxes to be warm, gracious, and in a humble posture of learning from one another."[8]

Clearly, a church is in many ways unlike a business organization. And yet Carter's prescription would be well received by most businesses. I am struck in this context by what I would call the "roominess" of the Three-Box Solution—that the framework is flexible enough to accommodate the circumstances of many different types of organizations. It is as available to a church as it is to a telecom firm or a maker of coffee-brewing equipment.

Second Box 3 Innovation: The Willow Creek Association

The Willow Creek Community Church grew steadily through the 1980s. Partly because it accomplished its growth during a time of overall declining church membership, it was seen as an interesting outlier and attracted the attention of pastors from other churches. They wanted to know what the secret of Willow Creek was and whether they could replicate it. Hybels found himself spending more and more time meeting with and answering the questions of pastors interested in creating similar success. A trickle became a stream and then a flood. In 1988, *Time* magazine ran an article about the Willow Creek phenomenon, causing a further escalation of attention and interest. "Eventually, we had hundreds of calls coming in. It was an unsustainable kind of conundrum."

A Proof-of-Concept Experiment

Hybels could have dealt with these pastors' curiosity about Willow Creek by politely deflecting their inquiries altogether or managing his calendar in a way that would have satisfied only a fraction of those who expressed interest. But he had always insisted that Willow Creek be "the church God intended us to be."[9] At every turn, he was open to it taking whatever shape events suggested it should—an enduring value that would persist over the decades.

So he conceived a solution to the unsustainable conundrum: what if they were to create an independent church-leader training organization? The idea of it being independent from (though related to) Willow Creek Community Church reflected his concern that the church should focus on the work of serving and growing the local congregation, and he wanted it insulated from potentially large distractions.

Nonetheless, it took several years for Hybels to create the Willow Creek Association as an independent organization. At first, he experimented with leader training as an ancillary church activity, holding conferences at regular intervals to help meet the demand from pastors of many denominations for education about the Willow Creek model. Beginning with twenty-six attendees in 1986 at the first such event, by 1992, the church was serving between four thousand and five thousand attendees from all over the world. Not surprisingly, the drain on the institution was considerable. The church could no longer deny that the conferences had grown to require the focused attention of a single entity whose sole mission was to educate pastors and churches.

Hybels formed the Willow Creek Association (WCA) in 1992 to create and deliver a curriculum on the Willow Creek way. He assembled a staff—some from the inside, some from the outside—and tasked them to build this new organization. The effort illustrates how well Willow Creek was able to balance its three boxes. Hybels created Box 2 hedges using a dedicated team (WCA) of insiders and outsiders. While the dedicated team was distinct and separate from the performance engine, the WCA borrowed a key asset from the Willow Creek Community Church—the base of knowledge and best practices that constituted the curriculum of "how Willow does it."

WCA's success was the result of creating a *hybrid organizational model*—a "separate but linked" organization to execute the Box 3 innovation.

TABLE 5-1

Willow Creek: Box 1 versus Box 3 thinking

WILLOW CREEK COMMUNITY CHURCH AND THE **WCA**

Components of the business model	Willow Creek Community Church (Box 1)	Willow Creek Association (Box 3)
Customer	• "Unchurched Harry/Mary" or "seekers" • Believers; church members	• Leaders of other Christian churches • Initial consumers: early adopters and innovators
Value proposition	• Exaltation (glorify God) • Edification (deepen spiritual belief) • Evangelism (reaching out to "unchurched") • Social action ("conscience to the world")	• Disseminate management innovation • Help churches thrive
Value chain architecture	• Use of music, drama, and multimedia in services • Scripture conveyed in a modern context • Seven-step strategy for reaching "unchurched"	• Seminar format for small groups • Curriculum focused on strategy and leadership • Global Leadership Summit
Competencies	• Theological training • Converting nonconsumers	• Thought leaders and practitioners • Expertise in teaching/ learning methodologies • Business expertise

All the while, the Willow Creek Community Church continued with its Box 1 business: preaching the word of God (see table 5-1).

The WCA had its own set of marching orders: training independent church leaders to build a new kind of church based on what Willow Creek had set out to be. The association shared its curriculum with all who were interested, eliminating the line of pastors waiting after services to pepper Hybels with questions. In time, the WCA would become a new species of evangelical phenomenon, spreading the Willow Creek philosophy to thousands of churches worldwide.

Jim Mellado Discovers Willow Creek

Around the time the conferences began to gather steam, a young evangelical Christian named Jim Mellado traveled to Seoul, South Korea, to compete as a decathlete, representing his native El Salvador in the 1988 Summer Olympics. While in South Korea, Mellado visited some Christian churches and was surprised to discover that Christianity had grown to be a significant religious force there. In 1952, at the time of the Korean War, "there were 0 percent Christians," said Mellado. "And now, by some estimates, more than 25 percent of the population of South Korea are Christians. Some of the world's largest churches are there. In fact, the world's *largest* church is there." He was impressed by the vitality of Korean Christianity and was "quite moved by the impact of what could happen when the church worked right and was actually fulfilling its mandate to serve people."

Some months after returning from Korea, Mellado was invited to visit Willow Creek Community Church. He was curious, so he went. "They had about fifteen thousand people attending, and while that seemed small compared to what I'd seen in South Korea, it was very large for the United States. I learned all about the church in a conference. I was there for two-and-a-half days, and that was that," he said.

In the meantime, Mellado's father was urging him to get an MBA. He already had an undergraduate degree in engineering, and his father, who was also an engineer, believed a business degree would complement his technical training. Mellado said, "So, almost to humor him, I made one application and I decided, 'Why not Harvard? I'm not going to get in anyway.'" But he did get in, and so he went.

During his time at Harvard, Mellado read an article by Peter Drucker describing some nonprofit organizations, including Willow Creek, that operated using enviably effective business methods.[10] Drucker used his examples to argue that many nonprofits were, in some areas, "practicing what most businesses can only preach." Mellado described his Willow Creek visit to some fellow students and word got back to Len Schlesinger, one of his professors. Mellado said, "He summons me to his office and quizzes me about the church. He says, 'Why is Peter Drucker interested in a church?' At the end of the conversation, Len said, 'Why don't we write a case study on this? I'm fascinated by it.'"

That's roughly how 1991 Harvard MBA Jim Mellado eventually joined the WCA. The various pieces of his experience—his Christian roots, his travel to the Olympics in South Korea, that earlier visit to Willow Creek, and later meeting Hybels while researching the case study—convinced him that he wanted the church to be at the center of his life's work. In 1992, Hybels offered him the chance to join the WCA, and he jumped at it. "I was the sixth employee," he said. At the end of 1993, he became its president.

An MBA for Church Leaders

The mission of the WCA was, said Mellado, "to help churches thrive. And the way we did that was by equipping church leaders . . . to be the catalytic mechanism to spur innovative thinking inside their churches." The founding idea of the WCA was that as the leadership goes, so go the churches. It therefore sought to produce better, more creative church leadership.

The most difficult concept for a traditional church to grasp is the counterintuitive mission deeply embedded in Willow Creek's model: that it is a church *designed for the members it doesn't yet have*—the nonconsumers—rather than for the faithful who already have joined. Willow Creek's focus on nonconsumers over consumers illustrates the difference between Box 3 and Box 1. Box 3 thinking materializes opportunities that exist but may not be visible.

While Box 1 thinking is comfortable and unthreatening, Box 3 thinking can seem contrarian. Indeed, when the Willow Creek case study was first discussed in class, one of Mellado's fellow Harvard MBA students noted that the church's program for reaching out to nonconsumers was like "taking business-class, frequent-flyer, million-mile-club kinds of people who fly all the time and pay full fare and asking them to sit in coach. And then taking first-time flyers—people who are afraid to fly—and putting them up in first class so they can have the absolute best first experience of flying in an airplane."

But Mellado points out that the early Christian church grew from a handful of Christ's disciples to three hundred million members as quickly as it did by serving the unchurched first and foremost. The church that Hybels originally envisioned was unique for its missionary spirit. The work of the WCA was to underscore that mission of service and outreach and to present the future-building Willow Creek model as logical and creative rather than jarring.

The other core aspect of Willow Creek's success was that its founders built it around a strategy. "*Strategy* and *church* were two words that hardly ever mixed," said Mellado. Some people, including business professors and students, tried to suggest that applying business disciplines to spiritual pursuits was inappropriate, that there was an important distinction to be made between selling Nike sneakers and selling religion. Religion was private and personal, and matters of faith were not subject to strategy.

Hybels disagreed. While the act of deciding whether to accept religion or convert from one faith to another might be deeply personal, the work of providing seekers with information and experience on which to base their decisions was surely amenable to strategy. Hybels said, "I happen to think that meeting the spiritual, physical, emotional, and cognitive needs of people through the church is a lot more important than selling shoes. But [I can't] just divorce myself from my brain and let no strategy exist, waste resources, waste people's time, and have no intentionality."

Willow Creek was all about intentionality. While the church accorded great respect to a seeker's private decision about taking or leaving the offer, in all other matters that might help shape the decision, strategy guided every aspect of creating the offer. Importantly, however, Willow Creek did not adulterate the substance of the Protestant belief system on which the church was founded. But because the WCA would attract pastors from many different Christian denominations, its curriculum was not mainly devoted to theology but rather to the church's innovations in the areas of worship, outreach, and effective church management and stewardship.

I cannot emphasize enough how unusual an organization the Willow Creek Community Church was at the time of its founding. Certainly some of its uniqueness owes a debt to Hybels's early business experience and training. But at the heart of Hybels's vision was his insight as a teenager that there was a growing population of nonconsumers of religion and, worse, that many churches responded to their plight with surprising indifference. It was a problem that in 1975 had cried out to be solved. The WCA would take the solution to a new level.

The surprising power of the WCA idea—especially since Hybels initially conceived it as a way to free himself from a growing set of distractions—was that it had the potential to become a viral instrument. The WCA team would build a global network of pastors trained to be leaders and innovators. The network would then become a force multiplier for Willow Creek's appeal to the unchurched, but with each pastor adding something new to the mix.

Finding the Early Adopters

As the WCA took shape, Mellado encountered the work of a social scientist and communications theorist named Everett M. Rogers. Rogers had developed a groundbreaking framework for understanding how various innovations are diffused and adopted. (He is credited with originating the term "early adopters.")[11] Mellado sought him out and invited him to come see what the WCA was trying to do. "He spent a day at the WCA and said, 'You've been given a gift. It's amazing! . . . Because Willow Creek is such a breakthrough innovation, it's a magnet. So you don't have to go to other churches to teach them about how you do it. You have effortlessly become a 'diffusion network.' They're coming to you!'"

Still, said Rogers, there were important distinctions to be made among the many who were flocking to Willow Creek. He advised that if the WCA could target those among the interested churches and pastors who were most likely to be innovators and early adopters, it would accelerate the rate of diffusion of Willow Creek's innovations.

Using this insight, Mellado methodically identified pastors and churches that appeared to be relatively more adventurous and risk tolerant. He said, "We began to look at the characteristics of innovative kinds of organizations and people: They tend to be more educated. They tend to have [churches] of a larger scale. They tend to be located around high-communication cosmopolitan centers. The pastors tend to [be information gatherers who] go to conferences and seminars."

Mellado said the WCA actively pursued those who were the most adventurous "not because we didn't care about the rest, but because we had limited resources. We knew we could reach the rest only by reaching the innovators and early adopters." So the WCA designed its marketing strategy to appeal explicitly to the most innovative leaders and churches.

Many of those who experienced the WCA conferences and who continued over the years to practice and preach what they learned there have told Mellado that they felt a deeper kinship with the Willow Creek conferences than with their own denominational conventions. "That's because they're rubbing shoulders with innovators, and innovators tend to learn best from other innovators," said Mellado.

About one-third of the WCA membership is nondenominational, meaning that Willow Creek is their only connection to a parent organization. According to Mellado, the rest of the members run the gamut of Christian churches, representing more than ninety denominations.

The WCA's conferences and training programs on how to adopt and adapt the Willow Creek way were immensely successful for a long time. "We had fifteen years straight of 20 percent annual compounded growth rate of attendance and revenues at the association," said Mellado. "It was quite a run."

Third Box 3 Innovation: The Global Leadership Summit

But Box 2 exists for important reasons. During those fifteen years, the WCA inadvertently "created a little church-conferencing industry," said Mellado. As church leaders from around the country and the world attended WCA events, they too were inspired to share what they had learned. Eventually, some of the next-generation churches began doing highly innovative events of their own. Inevitably, this flowering of new blooms began to erode attendance at WCA events.

The WCA had been a Box 3 move in 1992. But the natural goal of every Box 3 venture is to become a Box 1 business. Once the organization scaled up and became a performance engine, Mellado's team executed several linear Box 1 innovations: a portfolio of specialized conferences and training programs for particular types of ministries: children's ministry, students' ministry, small-group ministry, arts ministry, and others. These brand extensions provided both novelty and additional revenues that allowed the program to continue flourishing. But by 2007, the WCA executive team had begun to believe it had to face up to the need to create something altogether new. That realization brought on a five-year period of transition and transformation.

As the Great Recession kicked in toward the end of 2008, attendance at the conferences declined sharply. The downturn coincided with—and made more abundantly clear—the reality that the WCA had thoroughly mined the market for educating church leaders in the Willow Creek way. "There were now thousands of churches that looked like Willow Creek," said Mellado.

The WCA faced difficult choices. It employed roughly 150 people, many of whom had spent more than a decade running events built on the legacy curriculum. With annual revenue and attendance declining by increments roughly comparable to the growth rate during its most successful years, the WCA was no longer able to support such a staff. In a Box 2 move, the WCA shed two-thirds of its people in three rounds of layoffs.

A Successor Innovation

Few churches have occasion to develop a portfolio-management discipline, but Hybels, well schooled in both Ecclesiastes and business thinking, has done that at Willow Creek. "We have quite a disciplined leadership rhythm throughout the course of the year," he said. "In January, I'll take my senior leaders away for three days. We review every single ministry of the church and we ask, 'What's going well?

What's not? What's had its day? What do we need to *stop* doing? And what new Box 3 things do we need to start?'" In fact, Willow Creek does this exercise twice a year, and that helps keep everyone focused on the importance of Box 2. The question of what to stop doing isn't left unanswered until a crisis strikes, which is too often the case in many businesses.

So it was a process rather than mere gut instinct or a lucky guess that had the WCA executive team thinking about what should come next for the association. The result: the Global Leadership Summit, a forum for presenting content that is far more outward looking and visionary than the relatively inward-looking curriculum of how to adopt the Willow Creek model.

The Global Leadership Summit seeks to offer WCA members exposure to a diverse array of world-class thought leaders and practitioners in the broad area of leadership. The underlying philosophy of the event was to be the opposite of insular—to shop for interesting ideas both within and beyond the world of the church. It was launched as an experiment, with no clear idea that it would be successful. As it happened, however, the event caught on and began its growth spurt in time to be ramped up even as the original WCA conferences were being phased out.

Mellado's passion for the Global Leadership Summit was to make it as open-minded in its choice of experts as Harvard had been in adding a business school case study about a church to its teaching curriculum. The criteria for presenters would therefore not be theologically driven but based solely on the quality of their ideas and unique perspectives. Speakers at the Global Leadership Summit have ranged from GE CEO Jeff Immelt to British Prime Minister Tony Blair to filmmaker, actor, and philanthropist Tyler Perry. In 2013, I was honored to address the summit on the subject of the Three-Box Solution.

Mixing Timely and Timeless

The product of Box 3 thinking is often a mixture of qualities that are both timely and timeless. In being timely, a great Box 3 innovation is created fresh from something new and different—a technology or a business model—in the moment from which it springs. But an innovation is most likely to succeed when it also embodies the deep, enduring values of the organization that creates it. This is part of what defines the Three-Box Solution. The model is a hybrid that draws both on ideas and practices that are utterly unlike the past and on values that retain their relevance over the generations—values that are timeless. It was clearly a nonlinear act for Willow Creek to create an event with no obvious churchly roots beyond the importance of leadership excellence to churches. But the summit was also true to the timeless values of Willow Creek—a strong commitment to reaching out to the world at large to welcome and understand it and a firm belief that even churches must embody operational and strategic coherence.

"A leader has to constantly keep the three boxes in balance," said Mellado. "You have to eat while you dream. It is not Box 1 or Box 2 or Box 3. To be a leader is to be in all three boxes. And as a leader, you have to know how to operate differently in each box. In Box 1, you have to use a microscope. But in Box 3, you should put the microscope away and use a telescope. Seamlessly moving across the boxes is the hallmark of an effective CEO."

Today, the WCA has more than seven thousand member churches in ninety countries. The Global Leadership Summit is held once a year at Willow Creek's large headquarters facility in South Barrington, Illinois. In 2014, the summit attracted 225,000 total participants, including a live audience of 95,000 church leaders and 130,000 others worldwide via global telecast.

Willow Creek has become the product of the Three-Box Solution. If Hybels's definition of church had been conventional and if he had not been open to Willow Creek becoming the church he believed God intended, none of these innovations would have happened. More important, however, is that Willow Creek institutionally accommodated the cycles of preserving, forgetting, and creating. To each of these there was a season.

The church was able to translate its mission, activities, and innovations into executable Box 1 processes. The processes were subject to ongoing Box 2 scrutiny, and a culture of open inquiry developed, making space for further Box 3 experimentation.

Always Be Balancing

The spirit of ongoing open inquiry is a crucial by-product of the Three-Box Solution. It is essential to what I describe as a "change-ready culture." Change typically is both most challenging and most often resented and resisted when it occurs too infrequently, usually as the result of a crisis. The Three-Box Solution is no more or less than a method for *continuous* change, practiced in small daily ways that over time produce dramatic differences and a sustainable strategic posture.

I have had the opportunity to observe the evolution of a change-ready culture at Tata Consultancy Services (TCS), which over the years has transformed its business model and strategic and operational focus on numerous occasions. As a result, it has not just kept up with the curve but has been able to define its steepness. Had TCS not operated in that way, it would have had neither the foresight nor the courage to divest its call-center operations (as I described in a sidebar

Hiring beyond Box 1

At around the same time Tata Consultancy Services was divesting its call-center business, it was also preparing for a more strategic future by reinventing a department that many organizations erroneously see as a humdrum, do-not-disturb corner of the organization. CEO S. Ramadorai (known as Ram) and others at TCS were beginning to question the design and mission of TCS's human resources (HR) function, which hitherto had been a largely back-office administrative activity. According to Ram, "[The HR group] played little or no role in scouting for new talent."[12] That needed to change or else TCS would perpetuate HR competencies that were correct for call-center body shopping but wrong for its higher ambitions.

Because the trajectory of the business aimed at becoming more central to customers' strategic objectives, TCS needed to grow the volume of strategic skills represented throughout its workforce. Moreover, it would require not only diverse and advanced IT skills, but also sophisticated consulting skills and a keen understanding of competitive issues in the various industry sectors in which TCS would bid for contracts. Added Ram, "Although the company had a systematized process for entry-level hiring, we did not have much experience in hiring the more senior people we needed from sectors outside IT who would bring in domain and consulting skills and add diversity to our employee base."

Ram saw that HR needed to be entirely revamped in order to make such a project successful. One gap stuck out in particular: HR and operations had been kept quite separate and "most HR managers had little or no operational experience." This was especially problematic "because one of the key functions in an IT business is allocating people to projects. The challenge is to match the person with the right skills to a project at the right time while minimizing the 'bench time' that someone spends between projects."[13]

in chapter 3). Bear in mind that the company took this action well before any obvious signs of trouble emerged, at a time when the business was growing rapidly.

Consequently, Ram chose an operational wizard for the task of overhauling the HR function. S. Padmanabhan, better known as Paddy, "was a mild, soft-spoken person who had worked for TCS for twenty years and had experience in building an operation from scratch."[14] But he was not fully persuaded by the offer. According to Ram, TCS "[was] perceived as body shoppers, a cost-arbitraging company with ordinary HR skills and competencies . . . Paddy thought this move would effectively sideline him, but I wanted him to take up the challenge and change things."[15]

So Ram gave Paddy latitude to create the HR function he would be proud to lead. TCS badly needed to become an organization capable of rapidly absorbing and integrating new learning. Paddy often put himself in the center of that challenge. For example, TCS was having difficulty landing the business of a large US client and Paddy wanted to understand the problem. So he traveled to meet with the client. According to Ram, "The client told [Paddy] that their employees had felt threatened by our proposal team—it was an 'all-male Indian team' while their workforce was all American and of equal gender. It was a lesson in the value of diversity and that is when we started hiring local sales people and stepped up the hiring of women in all geographies."[16]

Ultimately, Paddy rebuilt the HR group to focus its work in five areas: improving productivity, acquiring talent, retaining talent, developing more-skilled leaders, and planning for leadership succession. Each one of these areas is strategic and each enhances the prospects for the organizational practice of planned opportunism.

First under Ram and then under the leadership of N. Chandrasekaran, who was named CEO in 2009, TCS's sales grew from $500 million in 1998 to $12 billion by 2014—growth of twenty-four times over a fifteen-year period. The renewed HR function played a significant role in helping TCS grow. Had TCS not divested its call-center business, the work of the HR function might well have been consumed by the burden of continuously replacing call-center reps—not at all the right future.

Balance depends to a great extent on knowing who and what you are *now* and how that knowledge squares with your sense of the future. That is what allowed TCS to recognize that call centers were a mismatch with its core goals and timeless values—a path to the wrong future. But there's a big difference between having such an insight and being willing to act on it by shutting down a promising business. Doing that required strategic confidence and the decisive leadership of CEO S. Ramadorai. Call-center divestiture was a radical Box 2 move that cleared the way for other, equally important moves, such as the reinvention of human resources (see the sidebar, "Hiring beyond Box 1").

CEO Ramadorai retired in 2009 after a thirty-seven-year tenure with TCS. N. Chandrasekaran, known as Chandra, succeeded Ramadorai and continued the company's transformational journey. In the chapter 4 discussion of United Rentals, Inc. (URI), one of the things I noted was how circumstances compelled it to begin changing its strategy just as the Great Recession was setting in. That proved fortuitous to the extent that URI already had accomplished its cost-cutting measures in a thoughtfully targeted way before others in the industry had begun. Thus, even in the depths of the downturn, URI was able to make strategic investments toward its long-term goal of changing the nature of competition in its industry. The ability to navigate from change to change was enhanced by the fact that the company was regaining its confidence and developing a more change-ready posture.

TCS likewise was ready to make new strategic investments in the teeth of the Great Recession, starting in early 2009. Like URI, it worked to deepen its understanding of how a sophisticated digital organization might better serve its customers. Like Hasbro, it creatively speculated about future opportunities by reading weak signals in emergent technologies, including the equal parts promising and controversial "Internet of Things" consisting of pervasively networked devices whose embedded sensors continuously gather, analyze, and share information. As a result, starting in 2010, TCS launched a number of initiatives to advise clients on the opportunities inherent in digital business strategies. Like IBM, TCS has and continues to make significant bets on cloud and big data analytics.

The point to take away from this idea of change-ready cultures is that they are powered by balanced Three-Box Solutions that showcase a wide assortment of planned opportunism initiatives. And these initiatives are not simply ad hoc; they are programmatic. A perfect example is TCS's move to create an HR function designed around the essential mission to hire for the future, not just for the moment, or Mike Kneeland's meetings with employees in which he puts the change agenda of today in the context of demands that the future will place on URI. In that sense, you can reasonably infer that the Three-Box Solution doesn't require a change-ready culture; over time, it *creates* a change-ready culture.

Finally, before we move on to chapter 6, which is about the role of leaders in the Three-Box Solution, it is good to think back to chapter 1 and the example set by Brian Goldner of Hasbro. Goldner recognized the goal of achieving three-box balance as one of his fundamental responsibilities, making sure each week that he was allocating appropriate time and attention to each of the boxes.

As Jim Mellado observed, "seamlessly moving across the boxes" is the constant condition for the leader of a balanced enterprise. Like the real-estate salesmen in *Glengarry Glen Ross* who are told to "always be closing," leaders of sustainable businesses must always be balancing. The task requires more than nonlinear ideas and executable processes. It requires a portfolio of six behaviors, which I will describe next by looking at the leadership of the Mahindra Group.

Takeaways

- *Devoting time and creative energy to the problems of nonconsumers is a counterintuitive nonlinear strategy.* It's very easy for a business to focus exclusively on existing customers. But, as many churches learned during the long period of membership decline in the 1960s and '70s, unless members can be lured away from competitors—a zero-sum game—they have to come from the ranks of nonconsumers. Most businesses spend too little time thinking about the problems of people who are not already their customers.

- *Sometimes nonlinear leaps can be inspired by practices that are linear elsewhere.* In his adolescent years, one of Bill Hybels's key insights was to see the need to import the missionary model from overseas. McDonald's founder Ray Kroc was inspired to import assembly-line manufacturing techniques into restaurants, thereby innovating the fast-food business model. Having the vision to see relevance in strategies and models that exist in dissimilar domains is a form of Box 3 thinking. Beyond his founding insight to build a church for the unchurched, Hybels had the instincts of a "creative borrower."

- *Preserving, forgetting, and creating are part of a cyclical process of renewal.* Weather provides us with observable signs of seasonal change. Unless it buries itself in denial, an enterprise can learn to see the signs of cyclical change in the measurable performance of its various businesses, and the emergent trends revealed in weak signals and in the timeliness of its nonlinear Box 3 ideas. While the seasons change without much help from humans, businesses need formal mindfulness.

- *A discipline consisting of unsentimental Box 2 practices and processes is necessary to enable a pattern of cyclical renewal.* Yet businesses fall prey to both habit and sentimentality. The hardest question that many businesses never ask themselves is, what should we *stop* doing? For that reason, successful Three-Box Solutions require programmatic mechanisms for asking and answering that and other central Box 2 questions. Willow Creek, Hasbro, IBM, Tata Consultancy Services, and others are committed to achieving balance among the three boxes through a combination of operational processes, organizational structure, and management behavior.

- *Training is underrated, often designed ineffectively, and (for both reasons) often underutilized.* But when core values and successful execution of strategy are at stake, training is essential. Willow Creek's mission to convert nonconsumers to faith was important enough to warrant a four-week training program that left nothing to chance.

- *One of the many benefits of balancing the three boxes is that it produces a change-ready culture.* That's because Three-Box Solutions work as instruments of continuous change, often achieved in small, day-by-day increments. The more accustomed an enterprise is to thinking of change as an operational constant, the less it provokes discomfort and outright resistance.

TOOLS

Tool 1: Assess the Three-Box Balance in Your Organization

1. Willow Creek leaders retreat twice a year to review how well the organization is balancing the three boxes. What tools or actions within your organization focus attention on . . .

   - What's going well?

   - What's not?

   - What's had its day?

   - What can be created going forward?

2. What is your top management's mission for the next decade? Long-term growth targets? Profitability goals?

3. Describe the gap between where you are today and where you want to be in ten years.

4. Classify all your current projects into Box 1, Box 2, and Box 3.

Tool 2: Balance the Three Boxes in Your Organization

1. Will the current portfolio of linear (Box 1) and nonlinear (Boxes 2 and 3) innovations close the gap between where you are today and where you want to be in ten years?

2. If not, how would you rebalance the portfolio of linear and nonlinear projects in a way that would better close the gap?

3. What are the total resources you will allocate to gap-closing activities this year?

4. How much of these resources will be spent on Box 1 and how much on Boxes 2 and 3?

5. What mechanisms are in place to protect the resources earmarked for Boxes 2 and 3?

6. How well does your organization train its people in the things that matter most—your core values and the successful execution in the three boxes?

7. What is the rate of change in your industry?

8. What is the rate of change inside your company?

9. Is the rate of change inside your company faster than the rate of change in your industry? If it is, you are probably maintaining a healthy balance among the three boxes.

6

Leading Innovation

In chapter 5, we looked at creating a Three-Box Solution through the lens of process, illustrated by the purposefully designed systems and recurrent activities of Willow Creek Community Church. In this concluding chapter, we look at a half-dozen types of leadership behavior that contribute to achieving balance. These leadership behaviors are (1) avoiding the traps of the past, (2) being alert to weak signals, (3) building the future every day, (4) experimenting and learning, (5) practicing planned opportunism, and (6) investing in "the horse you can control" (see table 6-1).

I have chosen a fascinating organization as my laboratory for Three-Box Solution leadership conduct: the Mahindra Group, headquartered in India, which does business in a wide array of industries—from steel, automotive, and agriculture to finance and hospitality. Organizations of such great variety are knit together by leaders able not only to empower discrete divisions subject to very different industry norms, but also to assert shared values and principles that unify the divisions as a coherent enterprise.

TABLE 6-1

Six leadership behaviors in the three boxes

	Box 1 Manage the present	Box 2 Selectively forget the past	Box 3 Create the future
Avoid the traps of the past	No one working in the Box 1 performance engine thinks of the past as a trap. Instead, it is the gift that keeps on giving.	Box 2 clears away the clutter of the past, the old ideas and practices that crowd out new, nonlinear ideas–the future's raw materials.	The work of Box 3 is to provide for future growth–a mission strategically distinct from that of the performance engine.
Be alert to "weak signals" that may point to long-term trends and nonlinear shifts	Box 1 is devoted to the efficient, profitable execution of the current business. Since weak signals are emergent and ambiguous, they distract Box 1 from the core mission.	Box 2 strives to improve access to weak signals and unconventional opinions. To do that, it must eliminate the noise of obsolete ideas and activities and create protective structures, such as dedicated teams.	Box 3 needs mavericks and outsiders to identify weak signals and use them to generate nonlinear business ideas. Leadership must distill these into distinct points of view and sponsor actions to build the future.
Create the future as a day-to-day process and recognize that the future is *now*	In Box 1, the *present* is *now*. Innovation amounts to improvising within a well-defined frame to improve near-term performance. Focus is on optimizing the current business model.	The focus of Box 2 is to selectively forget aspects of the *past* that have outlived their usefulness and now stand in the way of moving boldly into the future. The trick is not to sweep everything aside; it is to preserve aspects of the past that remain relevant and valuable while still making room for what is new.	In Box 3, the *future* is *now*. The best ideas for the future are nonlinear—inconsistent with the past. Developing and executing nonlinear ideas requires dedicated teams that operate free of the dominant logic, practices, and structures of the Box 1 business. Insulate teams from interference but empower them to draw on necessary performance-engine resources.
Experiment and learn	Experiments in Box 1 are low in risk, fueled by hard data, and focused on the near term.	Box 2 eradicates traditional metrics that apply to the performance engine. Experiments are uncertain by definition, so their success can be judged only by the learning they produce.	Box 3 experimentation increases certainty in iterative steps by testing the validity of critical assumptions, leading to growing confidence or modifications or a timely exit strategy. The goal is to manage investment in a rational way. Therefore, leaders of Box 3 initiatives should be judged on their ability to learn and adapt quickly, not prodded toward short-term financial goals.

TABLE 6-1 *(CONTINUED)*

	Box 1 Manage the present	Box 2 Selectively forget the past	Box 3 Create the future
Practice planned opportunism to be resilient in the face of change	Even those who work in a robust performance engine should anticipate possible changes. Box 1 isn't meant to be static.	By continuously evaluating the relevance of established ideas and activities and divesting those that have lost their value, Box 2 ensures a firm's fitness to act on new opportunities.	Building a platform of new skills and capabilities and embracing the discipline of experimentation are perfect preparation for responding to change. You develop an evolving sense of where the future lies.
Invest energy in the "horse you can control," in order to influence the horse you can't control	The forces that can threaten Box 1 are relatively predictable. Hedge against economic ups and downs, labor disruptions, and regulatory changes.	Box 2 demands hard decisions about what to keep and what to divest. Focus on moves that advance circumstances you can control, such as hiring skills beyond those needed in Box 1.	Focusing on what you can control bears the greatest fruit in Box 3. Innovation may sometimes look like chaos, but it is built on experimentation, which emphasizes controllable factors and orderly (iterative) progress.

Perhaps most notably, Anand Mahindra, leader of the company since 1991, has fashioned a can-do culture that values maverick thinkers, welcomes outside influences, sees risk as a blessing, and hones the hard work of selective forgetting to a sharp discipline. He also practices planned opportunism at the enterprise level, equipping each of the company's diverse divisions with the capacity to control its own destiny, compete aggressively in the present, and work continuously to develop its future. Mahindra is a leader who embodies the Three-Box Solution in his own behavior and spreads it throughout the business.

Neither processes nor behaviors by themselves are sufficient to guarantee sustainable Three-Box Solutions; like muscle and bone, both are indispensable, interdependent elements. For example, you can look at Willow Creek and see that strong leadership helped make its institutional processes successful. And you will see in this chapter that the Mahindra Group relies on process just as it does on its leaders' mastery of the six critical behaviors.

At the Mahindra Group, the six leadership behaviors began with a Box 2 problem of nearly gargantuan dimensions: the end of the so-called License Raj system, under which the Indian government licensed and tightly regulated domestic businesses while excluding foreign competitors. That system, which had been put in place in 1947 when India gained its independence from Britain, was in many ways comparable to the Soviet-style, centrally planned economy. The government called the shots, determining who could be in business, what they could sell, in what quantities, and at what prices. Since every business operated thanks to a license from the state, competitive advantage, such as it was, consisted mainly of managing the firm's relationships with the government agencies that controlled its destiny.

License Raj was intended to allow Indian businesses to emerge and flourish under protected conditions, but it had the unintended effect of inducing complacency, limiting incentives for truly robust competition, and discouraging innovation. As such, it was the exact opposite of a market economy. But since India was closed to outside competitors, each business was at least on a roughly equal footing with all the rest.

While there had been occasional modifications to the License Raj regime, particularly during the 1980s, it remained largely intact until wholesale reforms were instituted in 1991, leaving almost every business at the bottom of a steep learning curve.

Post–License Raj, the Mahindra Group has become one of the most successful global corporations:

- As of 2015, the company's agriculture division had risen to be the world's leading maker of agricultural tractors, measured in units sold, unseating US-based rival John Deere.

- After functioning for decades as an assembler of Western auto-makers' vehicles for sale to Indian consumers and with no proven competency in designing cars of its own, the Mahindra Group's automotive division innovated a breakthrough SUV, called the Scorpio. Launched in 2002, it continues to outsell competing vehicles made by Ford, Renault, and others.

- Across the board, the Mahindra Group's results have been exceptional, especially when you factor in the global Great Recession. From 2003 to 2014, sales grew from $1.35 billion to $17 billion, a thirteenfold leap. Its stock went from $22 in 2002 to $1,418 in 2014, an incredible gain of 6,500 percent (share price converted into dollars).

None of this happened by accident. Anand Mahindra followed a path of balanced priorities in which present, past, and future each got its due. In the process, he helped transform his company from a complacent creature of License Raj into a sustainable enterprise fit for market competition.

Behavior 1: Avoiding the Traps of the Past

After Anand Mahindra graduated from Harvard Business School in 1981, he returned home to India to work in the family business. The Mahindra Group was then a sprawling but sleepy company serving its numerous industry segments. The newly minted MBA first went to work in the company's flagship steel division.

The steel sector at that time, said Mahindra, "was a very cozy industry" with only a handful of players, all of which produced steel of roughly comparable quality and price using the same methods and technology. The idea of innovating was foreign to the cultures of these companies. But beginning in the 1980s, the government decided to expand the sector by licensing producers that relied on dramatically less expensive induction furnaces rather than the capital-intensive arc furnaces that Mahindra Ugine Steel and the other incumbents used. "So all of a sudden, from an industry where there were five players, it suddenly mushroomed," said Mahindra, "because you can set up an induction furnace in your backyard!"

Thus, in India's steel industry, new technology created a crisis of the kind most domestic companies had been able to avoid: the sudden outbreak of a genuine competitive threat. Mahindra commented, "I landed in a company that had finished its best year and then suddenly had to compete—and didn't know how to spell the word *competition*."[1]

Looking back, Mahindra reckons that dealing with an influx of new rivals gave him a microcosmic head start in understanding the challenges India would face in 1991 when the License Raj system ended and real rough-and-tumble global competition began. What Indian businesses faced was nothing less than learning to compete from the ground up, which meant forgetting most of what they had taken for granted in the decades since 1947.

Any good project manager would advise that it's best to break projects of vast size and complexity into small, manageable chunks. As the saying goes, the journey of a thousand miles begins with a single step. But it is also important to choose that first step for the disproportionate impact it will have and for its potential to make subsequent steps proceed more smoothly. Often, project leaders choose so-called low-hanging fruit—something obvious and relatively straightforward that will quickly persuade skeptics that the project's overall goals are achievable after all.

Turning a Gift into a Bonus

By 1991, Anand Mahindra had moved up from the steel division to assume leadership of the entire Mahindra Group. As License Raj ended, the most urgent imperative was to shake the business out of its complacency as fast as possible. A company's past is often rooted deeply in its culture—comprising habitual processes, rituals, and belief systems—so, selectively forgetting the past can require shocking the culture out of its habits and expectations, allowing it to rise to the challenge of radically new circumstances.

Mahindra settled on a change that was bound to be difficult and controversial—an explosive mix of symbolism, cherished tradition, and employee entitlement—the annual Diwali bonus. Such bonuses are extra compensation given to workers on the occasion of a major Hindu festival. Although bonuses are generally understood to reward exceptional performance, over time Diwali bonuses came to be more like gifts. As such, Mahindra saw them as emblematic of the wide gulf between the level of complacency under License Raj and life in a normally functioning marketplace.

In short, the Diwali bonus was a hot-button tradition he could use to make a powerful point. The Indian economy was in shambles and the company was in trouble. Mahindra was not in a gift-giving mood. "The first time we had to give the bonus, I said, 'Why? A bonus for what?' And the answer was, 'A bonus because we have *always* given one.'" Mahindra shook his head and replied, "A bonus cannot be an entitlement. It is for *performance*. It is something *extra* given in exchange for *extra* performance." He canceled the awarding of the bonus.

The news festered in the company for a few days. Then Mahindra looked out his office window one afternoon and "saw this line of workmen sneaking out of the factory building and coming up toward me, screaming for my blood." Under siege, he held them off for four hours, finally agreeing to sit down with a delegation of workers the following day. In that meeting, he said, "We could point to the fact that the country was out of money, that the government had opened up and was allowing imports in [and] was allowing global players to compete in India. We could point to Indian companies that were already floundering. We were able to use the environment to emphasize that we had to forget the paradigms of the past. The new environment demanded a new set of processes and rituals to meet higher workforce productivity, where just showing up was insufficient. 'You're going to have to work for it. *Bonus* now means what it etymologically means!' That is how we were first able to make the organization [begin to] forget the past."

Leading with Steadfast and Visible Conviction

There's no question that to draw a line in the sand takes courage. But it is impossible to overstate the importance of such highly visible public displays of leadership, especially when they are grounded in reality and expressed with true conviction.

The Diwali bonus episode began a series of labor challenges that spanned a number of Mahindra Group divisions, including a three-month shutdown at an engine factory. These were predictable symptoms of a massive campaign of forgetting. Forgetting is never easy, and Mahindra's goal was no less than to replace the complacent legacy culture with a performance-driven culture.

Surviving this period of labor unrest, said Mahindra, "was a major turning point. Once we finished with that, we achieved a 120 percent rise in productivity." It was as if the fever broke. "We never looked back."

Behavior 2: Being Alert to Weak Signals

Weak signals are the raw material from which nonlinear ideas are formed. The relatively few, widely distributed (and mostly young) mavericks within your organization who are least influenced by the dominant logic of past success are, temperamentally, the people most likely to tune into weak signals. Therefore, a key leadership responsibility is to identify these mavericks and make sure their ideas are heard and valued (see the sidebar, "Tapping into Weak Signals").

Mahindra developed a reputation for tolerating maverick thinkers—people who sometimes clash or don't fit in well with their colleagues. His tolerance for such characters is almost entirely opportunistic. Mavericks see the world in ways others don't and thus are more likely to conceive of unconventional solutions. Unfortunately, they can be abrasive, and that often attracts more attention than does their brilliance, causing the business to lose out in the long run.

Learning Why Mavericks Matter

Mahindra was fortunate to learn, early in his tenure, the difference mavericks can make. Among Mahindra's various duties as head of the company was to oversee R&D across the divisions. In 1991, he encountered a difficult situation in the automotive division. The unit manufactured a six-seat Jeep version that typically served as transport for so many people—sometimes fifteen to twenty riders—that the chassis eventually would crack from the stress of frequent overloading. The volume of cracked chassis became a major problem.

Since the company's engineers couldn't change the way customers used the vehicles, they decided to design a new, more rugged chassis equal to the usage demands. But the new design was going to require new metal-stamping machinery that would cost the equivalent of $8 million. "In those days, that was an enormous amount," said Mahindra. "Nobody had the courage to authorize such capital spending."

The impasse was broken when Mahindra's deputy called his attention to a young man, Sandesh Dahanukar, who had the idea to develop a tubular chassis that would satisfy the heavy-duty design specifications but not require buying new metal-stamping machines.

Tapping into Weak Signals

Box 3 strategy is about trying to anticipate nonlinear shifts by reading weak signals—emergent and as yet unverifiable clues to what the future may bring. Weak signals should be thought of as uncommon wisdom. They are most likely to be observed by younger employees—those who are new to your organization or who work at its fringes—or by complete outsiders. Tapping into the insights of such people will require a distinctly Box 3 process that can take one of two forms: a *handpicked task force* or a *democratic free-for-all*.

The task force approach. When I was the chief innovation consultant for GE from 2008 through 2009, we designed a process to brainstorm Box 3 ideas aimed at growing GE Healthcare's business in India. In its Box 1 business, GE Healthcare makes complex, high-performance, medical imaging equipment—X-ray machines, CT scanners, ultrasounds—that it sells at a high price to India's top hospitals. The company's top management team can formulate effective strategies for these products because Box 1 is concerned with current customers and current competitors, about whom there are many established sources of objective data to guide decision making.

Box 3, on the other hand, is about building a future business serving nonconsumers (in this case, rural Indians with limited access to health care) and competing against nontraditional rivals, including small local players. Rich sources of unambiguous data are not available about the future. To address this challenge, we assembled a Box 3 task force whose members were chosen carefully—twenty executives from inside the company, though not necessarily at the top of the organization. Of greatest importance was that each was a so-called maverick thinker and all were relatively young, most having worked for GE Healthcare for fewer than five years. We also chose twenty outsiders—hospital administrators, nonconsumers, health-care academics, government officials, and regulators.

The forty-member team spent a week identifying weak signals that suggested a variety of nonlinear shifts. From that raw material, the team brainstormed Box 3 ideas for "good enough" quality medical imaging devices to be produced at an ultra-low cost. Two things distinguished the team's output. First, it was able to easily identify and understand a wide variety of weak signals and nonlinear shifts. Second, it had very little vested interest in GE Healthcare's high-end medical imaging equipment.

The free-for-all approach. There is another potentially useful model for identifying and acting on elusive Box 3 insights, one that taps the wisdom of a well-defined crowd.

India's most valuable company, the IT services firm Tata Consultancy Services (which is discussed in chapters 3 and 5), uses a digital platform called Ultimatix to allow its three hundred thousand employees to share weak signals, fresh perspectives, and Box 3 ideas with TCS management and one another. TCS's innovation group, for example, uses the mobile-, social-, and cloud-enabled Ultimatix to run contests and jam sessions and to solicit and discuss ideas on specific Box 3 challenges. In the latter category, a typical question might be, How can TCS create nonlinear business models in the fields of health and education in emerging economies?

With a potential respondent base of three hundred thousand, even a small fraction of participants could overwhelm human screeners. But TCS has developed a software application that sifts through huge volumes of responses, identifies common themes, and zooms in on the most promising potential growth strategies.

Both of these approaches for identifying new ideas are valid under the right circumstances. The task force approach is probably best suited for a relatively more narrow inquiry—for example, How can our high-end imaging products be deconstructed into low-cost versions that are affordable and accessible to nonconsumers? The free-for-all serves as a good all-purpose collection point for a nearly limitless variety of random observations and ideas that can be auditioned, vetted, further refined, and eventually acted upon. It's conceivable that both strategies could be used in combination. Ideas gleaned from an Ultimatix-style system might be refined by a task force, or the output of a task force might require feedback from the crowd.

Trusting in a Calculated Risk

"We allowed Sandesh to experiment with $15,000 in seed capital," said Mahindra. "We staged the risk in three installments. The worst that could happen is we'd lose $15,000. But if we can't trust mavericks like Sandesh, we will never forget old ways of doing things. We'll never embrace and pull off change. We were able to give him that kind of money, and at each successful milestone down the road we gave him more. And right away that cured all the chassis-cracking problems. It was a very big triumph, because here was this seemingly intractable problem [that demanded] a huge investment. And we had found a way to solve it by trusting this guy."

According to Mahindra, during Dahanukar's tenure in the company, "he was never able to work well with others. But people knew that I had this tolerance for such personalities." Mahindra had Dahanukar report directly to him to insulate Dahanukar from the pressures applied by dominant logic. (Recall from chapter 3 how the new monkey, without similar "air cover," was quickly brainwashed by the old monkeys.)

In the end, investing $45,000 in an unconventional solution saved Mahindra & Mahindra nearly $8 million. The experience embedded in Anand Mahindra an appreciation for the value of calculated risk taking by betting on mavericks. And his willingness to listen to their unconventional ideas percolated through the company's leadership culture and even beyond, because once creative mavericks learn that their ideas can win acceptance at the highest reaches of the business, they express them more often and with greater confidence.

In a 2014 commencement address Mahindra gave at the Indian Institute of Management, Ahmedabad, he exhorted graduates to take risks like the ones he took with Sandesh Dahanukar. "I have found that the days that I see now as wasted days of my life were those when

I didn't take an acceptable risk that I could have conceivably taken, when I didn't ask myself if there was a new and different way to do what I was doing, when I didn't set my sights as high as I possibly could have."[2]

Behavior 3: Building the Future Every Day

Mahindra's first several years in charge of the company were all about turning Box 1 into a well-functioning engine of competition. Across India, businesses accustomed to having the government make their most important decisions for them had to learn how an open marketplace worked. To be sure, it was heavy lifting for all of them. "There are times in a company's history when you will overspend time and energy on one of the boxes," says Mahindra. "Given that we were coming out of the License Raj, our primary focus in the early 1990s was to improve performance in the core businesses—typical Box 1 fare."

For example, the License Raj system specified production quotas that factory workers were often able to achieve in only four hours of effort a day. Mahindra said, "We had to make the company realize what a 'pull' system is—that you deliver according to the market needs . . . not simply ration out products according to some predetermined, government-imposed quota. Quotas were out!"

Mahindra drove high performance in Box 1 by establishing stretch goals for productivity, business process reengineering, and short-term financial targets, and aligning metrics and incentives with measurable results in all three areas. By the mid-1990s, the Mahindra Group was prospering well enough to think about the future. And in any case, said Mahindra, "leadership is about balance. We have to learn to operate in all three boxes at once."

Federal Structure

The future is shaped by the actions you take *today*. Breakthrough business model innovation can happen *tomorrow* when leaders implement breakthrough organizational design *today*. It's quite likely that Anand Mahindra's greatest Box 3 organizational innovation is the *federal structure* he devised for the Mahindra Group in 1995. The federal structure prepared the company to pursue breakthrough innovations he never could have imagined when he put it in place.

The structure had three distinguishing characteristics.

First, Mahindra had inherited a company that was functionally organized. For example, a vice president of manufacturing supervised factories across multiple divisions that competed in various industries and produced a diverse array of products. It is easy to see how, under such a scheme, focus suffered when strategy was centralized. Federal structure reorganized the Mahindra Group into six sectors—automotive, auto components, farm equipment, financial services, software, and infrastructure—with each sector operating independently under the leadership of an empowered, accountable CEO. Management could focus single-mindedly on competing and growing within the industry sector, taking full advantage of the rapid growth India's liberalization unleashed.

Second, Mahindra pledged that once a business unit reached critical mass, it would be listed on the stock exchange. Investors could then buy shares in individual Mahindra Group units without also having to buy the rest. (To date, separately listed companies include Tech Mahindra, a software-services unit; Mahindra Finance, which facilitates tractor purchases by providing farmers with financing; Mahindra & Mahindra (M&M), the automotive and farm equipment sectors; Mahindra Lifespace Developers, a real-estate development unit; and Club Mahindra, a time share vacation hospitality business.) This is in sharp contrast to a conglomerate, a multibusiness organization whose stock price reflects the combined value of its business units. Modern finance theory attaches a "conglomerate discount" since investors can more efficiently diversify their portfolios. A federation, on the other hand, is a collection of independently listed companies, each focusing on one area but all tied together by a common owner.

Third, in Mahindra's federal system, the corporate center doesn't just sit back and count the money. It provides "tying together" services by facilitating knowledge sharing across the portfolio of companies; leveraging operating synergies in R&D, procurement, and manufacturing; and acting as the custodian of values that every operating company shares. In these respects, Mahindra makes two key distinctions between his federal approach and the practices of private-equity firms (PEs), which own rosters of independent companies of various lineages. To quote Mahindra, "PEs turn companies around through financial reengineering. We do it the hard way, through strategic and operational transformation. There is another difference: we take the long view. Venture capitalists usually have a vesting period of seven years. For us, that would be a grave error. In Club Mahindra, had we taken the classic PE approach in the seventh year and sold out, we would have lost the opportunity to transform a $5 million investment into a $1 billion business."

The federal structure provided the business units with liberating autonomy but also with enough governance to knit them together— via shared purpose, values, resource sharing, accountability, and Anand Mahindra's leadership—across dramatically different sectors. In other words, they each had distinctive agendas defined by their industries but enough kinship that they were family, as opposed to a bunch of random strangers gathered at a bus stop.

By creating a structure that rationally allocated areas of focus, leaving management focus to the unit CEOs and goal setting, knowledge sharing, and overall governance to the federal center, "[o]ur goal was to convert the 'conglomerate discount' into a 'federation premium,'" said Mahindra. "Unlike the conglomerate structure, eventually our vision was to create a federation of independently listed companies, each one subject to the market test and market discipline."

Mahindra's experience shows that structural innovations can be nonlinear. If the future is to be created daily, a business must be designed to allow that to happen with the least possible structural friction.

Creating Overarching Strategic Focus and Purpose

Architecture isn't all that's required. Despite Mahindra's best efforts to create empowered, autonomous divisions, by the year 2000, he was concerned that the market wasn't properly valuing the company as a whole, and some units were underperforming. After gathering outside opinions, which ranged from darkly gloomy to optimistic, he realized that he was likely the cause of some of the company's marketplace challenges. "Obviously, I was not communicating the levers of value that we were building" Mahindra said. His initial conclusion was that he needed to find a way to improve communications, both internally and externally. However, further analysis convinced him that there was a lack of strategic clarity across the diverse divisions.

To do this and to express the company's core purpose and values, in 2002, Mahindra launched what came to be known as the Blue Chip Conference, an annual event for company executives that would articulate an aspirational goal for the coming year. In doing this, he put himself and the contemporary Mahindra Group in closer alignment with the company's founding principles circa 1945 (two years before Indian independence). In essence, the Mahindra Group of that era wanted to be a different kind of company—to value the dignity of work and workers, to profit while behaving ethically, and to contribute to the building of India's global reputation by creating products that were second to none.

The Blue Chip Conference has become a yearly platform for recommitting to this idea of being a different kind of company. The conference agenda cuts across industry sectors and sets expectations around themes, such as customer focus and global leadership, and hard targets for revenue growth from recently innovated products and services. And it sets stretch goals for future performance. From the launch of the conference—ironically, in the very year the Mahindra Group was delisted from the Bombay Stock Exchange (it was reinstated in 2007)—the company began a period of unprecedented growth.[3]

Moreover, by articulating a shared agenda that cuts across the six diverse sectors, the Blue Chip Conference serves as a demonstrably coherent way of explaining the company to itself. Thus, divisions and lines of business that spend much of their time entrenched in their own sector priorities, operating under the impression they have little in common with the other divisions, have the opportunity to see that they are part of something larger, with meaning and purpose beyond the sum of their parts.

Finally, the conference is a useful way of showing the fruits of change over time within the context of an almost seventy-year-long commitment to core values. And it asserts a clear direction for future innovations. As such, it reinforces the cyclical essence of the Three-Box Solution.

Behavior 4: Experimenting and Learning

The most notably successful product innovation to come out of M&M is the Scorpio SUV, launched in 2002. The Scorpio design effort was the division's inaugural effort to create an original vehicle. Until that point, M&M had been a licensed manufacturer of Jeep for the Indian market. As such, the division typically followed a recipe provided by its multinational partners, though it sometimes tinkered modestly with the recipe to localize for Indian preferences and usage requirements.

To be sure, these partnerships had taught the company to be a highly competent and efficient manufacturer. But to attempt an original vehicle design was a project of far greater magnitude than anything the company had ever done, filled with equal parts exhilaration and risk.

In 1993, anticipating this kind of move, Anand Mahindra had hired Pawan Goenka, a fourteen-year veteran of Detroit and General Motors, to lead R&D at M&M. While at GM, Goenka had specialized in engine design, though not, he said, the entire engine. "I specialized in certain *portions* of engines. So when I came to Mahindra, it was to look at the whole automobile. This was a total change of career."

Transitioning from the component level to the vehicle level excited Goenka, and Mahindra promised him complete freedom to run automotive R&D as he saw fit. "What got me to Mahindra was the fact that there were signs of the Indian automotive industry veering into the second phase of its evolution," commented Goenka.

Before the Scorpio project came along, the focus of R&D at M&M was primarily on making incremental improvements to vehicles produced under license. If Goenka had begun to reconsider the wisdom of leaving Detroit, doubt vanished when the Scorpio project materialized in 1997.

During one of his plant visits, Anand Mahindra was shown a sketch for an SUV (that would become the basis for the Scorpio). The sketch was dreamed up by a twenty-six-year-old design-school graduate, Shyam Alepalli, who had never before created a car. Mahindra said that when the young designer showed him a picture of the Scorpio,

"I remember that something in my gut was piqued, and I said, 'You know, what we're looking at here is the future of the company.'" Recalling that incident, Mahindra reflected, "[Shyam's] boss told me, 'This guy can't get along with anybody.' The moment he told me that, it was like some light went on in my head. I said, 'Perfect. If he can't get along with anybody, he is probably like Sandesh and I'll give him a shot.'"

Mahindra was the third generation of his family to lead the company. With his Harvard MBA and a distinctly modern outlook on strategy and operations, he hoped Scorpio would help him update both the image and the performance of what was then a fifty-plus-year-old business.[4] M&M's reputation in the automotive sector rested mainly on its production of Jeeps for use in rural settings. In those agricultural regions, customers best knew the Mahindra brand for the rugged tractors the company made. But its vehicles had relatively low market penetration in urban settings where multinationals held sway, and the company was not known for automotive innovations.[5] Scorpio would change that.

Linear or Nonlinear?

According to Goenka, from the start, there were two possible innovative directions in which to take the division's first original vehicle: Box 1 or Box 3. Or, as he described the options, "trying to do better what others were already doing or else doing something totally different."

Although some within the company favored taking a conservative "do the same thing better" approach, Goenka, given his background, thought it unlikely that Mahindra could beat the Detroit automakers at their own game. They would need to create not only an unprecedented vehicle, but also a new way of playing the game.

"Don't try and take the traffic head-on," said Goenka, "because the chances that you will win are not very high. You will have to divert the traffic [by coming out] with a product that in the Indian context would serve a new segment where nobody is present today."

M&M had plenty of experience with the rugged Jeep vehicles that are the antecedents of today's SUVs. But as of 1997, there had never been a sleek, modern, Indian-designed SUV, one that a wide variety of consumers would be attracted to and could afford to buy. And the ultimate idea from a marketing standpoint was to give the M&M brand a more cosmopolitan appeal *and* launch an SUV that eventually could compete globally.

Liberated to Go It Alone

The option of entering into a joint venture with Ford Motor Company went off the table at an early stage. Anand Mahindra described unveiling the Scorpio design to top Ford executives, including then-chairman Alex Trotman and vice chairman Wayne Booker. He had told them the development budget was the equivalent of $120 million, whereas Ford estimated that it would have invested more than a billion dollars to produce such a car in the United States. As Mahindra laid out the proposed Scorpio project, the Ford executives listened attentively, looked at clay models based on the young design-school graduate's original sketches, nodded their heads, and declared, "Not bad."

Then Booker suggested to Trotman that, given M&M's lack of experience developing original vehicles, Ford should send over dozens of its engineers to help with the project. Mahindra recalled that Trotman replied, "Wayne, we'll do no such thing, [because] if we send them thirty engineers, this car will come out looking, smelling, and costing as much as a Ford. And we don't want that . . . If these guys produce this car for the price they're claiming, then we better learn how to make cars from them."

Mahindra recalled this as a very fortunate, very liberating moment. "If they hadn't left us to jump in the deep end, what would have happened? We might have never learned [how] to build a car."

Looking back, Goenka remarked that Scorpio "showed us that we had the ability to start from nowhere—no people, no process, no design knowledge—and build all those capabilities. I think the rub-offs and collateral benefits from the Scorpio were huge not only for the [automotive division] but for the entire group."[6]

Experimenting with Experimentation

As I have stressed throughout this book, iterative experimentation is the key to resolving uncertainties, testing assumptions, increasing learning, and reducing risk in any Box 3 project. Whatever future Scorpio might create for the Mahindra Group, the project was sure to be risky. Consequently, experimentation would be an essential part of the Scorpio program. The experiments would include not only technical matters relating to the Scorpio design, but also the way the new vehicle would be marketed, capitalized, and produced.

Goenka devised a most unusual way of testing possible business model solutions for Scorpio: he sought approval to develop, at the same time as Scorpio, a new version of an existing vehicle to be called the Bolero—a somewhat smaller, lower-cost SUV that could serve as a test bed for Scorpio parts, technologies, design, manufacturing, and marketing strategies. So while Scorpio was certainly both the first SUV to be *conceived* in India and the first original Mahindra & Mahindra vehicle design, the Bolero was hustled into existence in large part to be a nexus of experimentation for Scorpio.

For example, said Goenka, M&M used Bolero to test its ability to design and manufacture original body panels, which the company previously had outsourced. "It helped us develop the confidence that we could do it ourselves," Goenka said. Indeed, many other parts and systems conceived for Scorpio were likewise first tested on Bolero. And every tested component was also—especially in the case of technologies to be provided by outside suppliers—a test of Scorpio's novel sourcing strategy (see later).

Although the Bolero project was initiated later than Scorpio, it arrived on the market a full two years before the Scorpio launch. One reason for fast-tracking Bolero so aggressively was to build in enough time for the various experiments it hosted to produce results and allow for needed improvements to be incorporated in Scorpio. "Three months would not have been enough [cushion] for experiments," said Goenka. The fact that Bolero was not a newly conceived product but an existing vehicle platform made possible the two-year window, during which it could function as a large-scale, in-market experiment for Scorpio's ultimate benefit.

Dedicated Team

A dedicated team of about 120 people was assembled to develop Scorpio. The group was divided into small cross-functional teams, and all were situated in an area that allowed them to be in close proximity to one another so that no conversation was more than a short walk away.[7] The entire team reported to Goenka. To build a cohesive team culture, the members, including its leaders, wore uniforms.

Apart from such symbolic enablers of team culture, there were other key factors driving the effort's eccentric design. Chief among them was that M&M had no track record in new vehicle design. Of course, if the company had no successes to brag about, neither did it have any failures to regret. In that sense, M&M had the advantage of beginning with a blank slate and no baggage. And before doing anything else, it would have to invent new rules for new vehicle design.

The best way to exploit a blank slate is with open-minded developers who embark on a project with as few preconceptions as possible. For that reason, the dedicated team's demographic skewed toward youth, with an average age of twenty-seven. Young people are less deeply invested in old ways of doing things and innately more willing to think and act differently. In order to get Scorpio right, the development team would have to be exceptionally creative, adaptive, flexible, opportunistic, and, above all, ruthlessly frugal.

Indeed, Anand Mahindra believed that the most radical innovation of the Scorpio effort wasn't so much technical as it was about changing the state of play. "It was doing more with less. *Frugal engineering* was the truly Box 3 aspect of Scorpio," he remarked.

Not Just Suppliers, but Development Partners

Both the requirement of radical frugality and M&M's lack of deep automotive design experience drove an experimental approach to sourcing relationships.

Detroit-style supplier relationships were both dictatorial and uncreative. Suppliers stuck to their subservient role. The automaker did all of the design work in-house and dictated specs to the supplier. The supplier then executed the designs exactly, with no opportunity to showcase original ideas or ingenuity. This sometimes cost automakers the loss of a supplier's ideas for delivering greater functionality less expensively, but that was the way of the world.

M&M, on the other hand, wanted to tap suppliers' ingenuity by enlisting them as design partners. Suppliers, therefore, were given unusual latitude, within a specified budget and performance thresholds, to create systems as they saw fit.[8] Examples of supplier partners included Korea's SL Corporation (formerly Samlip Industrial Co.) for the suspension system, India's Lumax Industries for automotive headlamps, and the US's Lear Corporation for automotive seats. Suppliers valued the opportunity to display their knowledge and to learn and stretch. According to Mahindra, "All the major systems were designed and engineered by suppliers . . . M&M's involvement was limited to specifying performance targets and costs and acting as an integrator in bringing together the components to create the final project."[9]

Fortunately for M&M, the timing worked to Scorpio's advantage. The Scorpio effort coincided with a period of overcapacity among automotive suppliers. According to Goenka, many large multinational suppliers of automotive technology—Behr, BorgWarner, Lear, and others—had opened facilities in India, hoping to attract business from US automakers. But the business had been slow to materialize. So, said Goenka, "they were very keen to develop a new product . . . expecting that Scorpio could grow into a large-volume play for them." And Indian suppliers were persuaded that their ability to succeed in the global market depended on developing strong engineering skills. "Many of the suppliers would tell you that the reason they're able to do engineering today is that they worked with us fifteen years ago and had to learn engineering," Goenka continued.

In this and other ways, M&M was able to develop highly collaborative supplier relationships that nonetheless stayed within its frugal budget. Indeed, the company leaned heavily on suppliers to hold down costs. And the fact that these relationships were transparent and collaborative allowed for a high degree of two-way communication between suppliers and M&M.

There were two motives behind the decision to grant suppliers such creative autonomy: to compensate for M&M's lack of key skills and to enlist suppliers as genuine partners in finding ways to hold down costs. M&M's head of strategic sourcing, Johnny Mapgaonkar, described this give-and-take: "If they could not deliver on a contract, we were happy to renegotiate. Whenever they returned to us with increased costs, we cooperated with them to find a solution that worked within the budget. The process was initially difficult because they were not used to auto companies listening to their advice . . . but over time they realized that we wanted to cooperate. We later realized that suppliers would approach us [on their own initiative] with cost savings!"[10]

The cost to develop Scorpio may have been one-tenth of what a big automaker would have invested, but it was still the biggest bet the Mahindra Group had ever made. "You have to forget that you have never spent this much money on any project before," said Mahindra. "You have to forget that you don't have any of the competencies and gateways and processes to build a car. You just have to have a very, very burning desire to transform and to get into another orbit."

Expanding M&M's Market

One higher orbit Anand Mahindra wanted to reach was reputational. His burning desire with Scorpio was to break free from M&M's limiting association with rugged rural vehicles. Not that there was anything wrong with serving rural customers, but modern, cosmopolitan India—and beyond—offered a wider, more affluent market to crack. Bolero was able to play a further experimental role in testing the appeal to India's urban consumers of a well-designed, well-featured SUV.

Though Bolero was smaller, less expensive, and not as finely appointed as Scorpio would be, it was designed to be stylish and comfortable and at least as much fun as functional. And it was a test of new marketing approaches that emphasized a more subtle set of messages and concepts than M&M was accustomed to using. Previously, said Goenka, the company's automotive marketing had been "very generic," focused more on function and utility than on style and sizzle. Bolero broke new ground by inverting those virtues and beginning to establish credibility with buyers in urban centers.

Before the Scorpio launch, M&M concluded it was best not to highlight the Mahindra brand but instead to make it dramatically subordinate to the name of the car. In all advertising, said Goenka, "we called it the Scorpio. Then, sort of below in fine print, 'by Mahindra.' But it was never the 'Mahindra Scorpio' or the 'Scorpio by Mahindra.' And Scorpio TV commercials tried to capture the aspirational feel of a 'typical commercial for Rolls Royce,' which the Indian public connected to very well."

The Scorpio marketing team also decided not to call it an SUV. A market for SUVs had not yet developed in India, and Goenka said the term would have meant relatively little to Indian consumers: "Instead, we just called it a car."

Goenka, with his roots in engine design, took pride in Scorpio for another reason; it was the first car in India to offer an engine of greater than 100 horsepower. "I think we had 109 horsepower at the time, which was unheard of in India in the mass market," he commented.

Practicing frugal engineering, the high-quality, low-cost Scorpio was offered at a price of 30–40 percent of competitors' vehicles. In January 2003, it was named the "Car of the Year" by three separate organizations.[11] In the first eighteen months after Scorpio launched, Indian consumers snapped up nearly thirty-five thousand of the cars. Most of the buyers were urbanites, and Bolero was eventually repositioned to play an aspirational role for rural consumers. Scorpio continues to outsell competitors in India, and it has expanded into many other markets, including those in Asia, South America, Europe, Africa, and Australia.

Scorpio wouldn't have happened without Anand Mahindra's gut instinct about the Mahindra Group's future. It was pure entrepreneurial risk taking and, as Goenka observed, it defied the meticulous calculations of conventional business planning. At the time, he said, the thinking boiled down to this: "We don't care what the IRR [internal rate of return] is. We don't care what the NPV [net present value] is. We don't care whether we can afford it or not afford it. But if we don't do it, we know we won't [continue to] exist."

Finally, like Mahindra, Goenka sees Scorpio as a full 360-degree innovation. It was a new product category aimed at a new market, relying on a new development strategy, radical cost goals, and a new business model. "We used Bolero as an experiment and learned a lot before placing the bigger bet on Scorpio. A lot of people think of Scorpio as a product innovation," he said. "It is a lot more than a new product. We managed to create in Scorpio a symphony between the product and the market. We invented a new business system. And that is what made it succeed."

Behavior 5: Practicing Planned Opportunism

One of the qualities I have noticed in Anand Mahindra is that when he addresses problems or opportunities, he doesn't think of them in isolation. He looks beyond a problem—or, indeed, an opportunity—to the matrix of conditions and circumstances that have made its existence possible.

A good example is how he approached the problem of the marketplace placing too low a value on the Mahindra Group's various businesses, both separately and together (as mentioned earlier in this chapter). Mahindra wanted not simply to fix a problem, but to understand on as many levels as he could what had made it possible.

For instance, among other conditions, he identified his own lapses as a leader and communicator as contributing factors. It took a capacity for humility on his part to accept personal responsibility. But he didn't merely change his own behavior; he went further to identify a lack of strategic clarity across the company. He then proposed a mechanism, the Blue Chip Conference, to sharpen the focus of every division on key strategic priorities. As a result, the Blue Chip Conference became a way not only to fix a problem, but also to prepare for whatever challenges or opportunities the future might bring.

Mahindra's unusual thought process reveals the importance of planned opportunism. Relatively speaking, fixing a problem is a low-value activity, whereas changing the conditions that lead to a problem is at the heart of planned opportunism. Over time, addressing particular problems becomes an opportunity to more ambitiously change the game.

In that context, Mahindra's decision in 1993 to hire Pawan Goenka to remedy M&M's troubling lack of automotive design expertise was a prescient step toward a much more wide-ranging transformation of the business: to build an increasingly confident engineering capability over time. This, in a sense, is not unlike Keurig's decision to hire Kevin Sullivan, with his GE background, to build up Keurig's capacity for product innovation in the demanding consumer market. Such foresight is an essential aspect of planned opportunism. You are looking around the corner to a future need. In 1993, four years before the start of the Scorpio effort, Mahindra was anticipating an opportunity that had not yet arisen. When it did, Goenka was eager to take it on.

But Goenka conceded that when he returned to India after his fourteen years at General Motors, with its billion-dollar R&D budget and army of twenty thousand engineers, he was not quite prepared for the state of M&M's R&D: a shed housing fifty engineers. He commented, "I must admit that the starting point was a lot less than what I had imagined."[12]

Fortunately, in the early 1990s, Anand Mahindra had toured ambitious research centers, such as Xerox's PARC and Chrysler's R&D facility in Auburn Hills, Michigan. And he was struck by the way the physical design of such facilities, with the cafeteria as their hub and de facto commons, stimulated spontaneous, casual interactions among engineers. Mahindra said, "'I was told that it was to create an environment where engineers from various departments can share notes when they eat.' That was when the automotive world was moving toward simultaneous engineering in product development."[13] He quickly grasped the value of allowing for cross-pollination among creative types and hatched a dream to replace the humble shed with a new research facility that could duplicate the stimulating environments and creative encounters he observed at US research centers. The idea was to build a central facility that would gather M&M's main automotive engineering force in one location—a fitting enabler for creative collaboration and serendipitous insights.

After beginning development in 2005, Mahindra Research Valley (MRV) finally opened in 2012 in Chennai, India. By 2015, MRV had 2,600 engineers across four domains: auto product development, farm product development, power train engineering, and advanced technologies. MRV is another instance of planned opportunism—building a platform of capabilities that allowed M&M to pursue new directions. The returns on this investment included a 20 percent faster pace of development from initial concept to product launch, the capacity to work on many more projects simultaneously, and more engineering development in-house, with less reliance on outside consultants. With the help of MRV's engineers, M&M introduced successful new

Planning for the Unpredictable Future

The success of Anand Mahindra as a leader and the Mahindra Group as an organization is due in no small part to their ability to prepare for futures they cannot predict through the application of planned opportunism:

- *The federal structure.* In devising a new structure, Mahindra created incentives for each of the Mahindra Group's diverse divisions to enjoy empowering autonomy and to be rewarded by the market for excellent performance. The federal structure changed the way the company viewed itself and outside stakeholders and observers evaluated it, and led to the profitable spinout and stock market listing of a number of Mahindra divisions.

- *A tolerance for mavericks.* Mahindra built the capability to spot, listen to, and respect the voice of mavericks. This chapter highlighted two such instances: Sandesh Dahanukar and Shyam Alepalli. As a result of Anand Mahindra's example, choosing foresight over personality became a best practice that spread across the organization. Executives learned to evaluate new ideas on the strength of their intrinsic potential, not the status of whoever had proposed them.

- *Box 2 becoming a corporate value.* Bringing fresh perspectives into any company has great value. Mahindra developed a practice of hiring retired senior executives from companies he admired and seeding them across the Mahindra Group. For example, Unilever's Indian operation had a policy of forcing retirements at age fifty-eight—"people who are all still feeling young." One such executive started by working part-time

products, among them the XUV 500, the fastest-selling SUV at the high end, and the Arjun Novo, a market leader in the tractor industry. "Engineers at MRV are working on twenty new products/variants and three new tractor platforms apart from developing many new technologies ranging from in-car infotainment, alternate fuels, emission and in the Mahindra Group's HR department. But he wanted to do more, so Mahindra made him CEO of one of the company's verticals. Mahindra said, "He had some rough edges and perhaps didn't endear himself to everybody, but he was outstanding in what he did. He just put the whole business right." Mahindra recruited many seasoned retirees still eager for a challenge. He commented, "Outsiders help overcome the forgetting problem. They are not bound by the status quo. Instead, they bring new ideas. We could have made a *Dirty Dozen* movie out of these people!"

- **The Blue Chip Conference.** The conference helped give annual shape and direction to every division's thinking about how to invest its time and energy. It also helped foster a sense of shared purpose across an enterprise that consisted of dramatically disparate pieces. That new sense of common purpose allowed for the possibility of bringing two or more divisions together around opportunities that they might not otherwise have glimpsed. For example, Mahindra Research Valley is now home to R&D for both the automotive and tractor divisions. "It is the only place in the world where automotive and tractor development takes place under one roof," said Pawan Goenka.[15]

- **A history of well-timed risk taking.** A leader who continually bets the company's future on an uncertain endeavor will sooner or later go too far. But with Scorpio, Mahindra picked the right bet at the right time. And he had anticipated the moment by putting in place enough talent, including Goenka, to lead a credible and creatively hedged development effort. Scorpio was a now-or-never bid for M&M to stake its claim in the global auto industry.

safety standards and light weighting the car [making the car lighter] to improve fuel efficiency," said Goenka.[14]

Besides MRV, M&M also opened a small technology center in Detroit (employing fewer than a hundred engineers) to absorb and leverage the experience of developed-world engineers, as well as a joint research center with SsangYong Motor Co. in South Korea. All three of these entities cooperate on numerous projects.

Clearly, both the Mahindra Group and Anand Mahindra have created enormous serendipitous value out of new conditions engendered by planned opportunism (see the sidebar, "Planning for the Unpredictable Future").

Behavior 6: Investing in the "Horse You Can Control"

You'll recall the metaphor in chapter 2 of attempting to balance on two horses, one that can be effectively controlled and the other one uncontrollable. The key is to know which is which. I first encountered this metaphor in Elizabeth Gilbert's 2006 book *Eat, Pray, Love*, but it has long been an important theme in business, where every management move and strategy must be weighed against the constraints and contingencies that affect it. Almost nothing at which a business attempts to succeed is without various kinds of constraints.

It is easy, of course, to become preoccupied with the infuriating intractability of circumstances beyond your control: "Why must this uncooperative horse be harnessed to my obedient one?" But the work of balancing the three boxes must focus as much as possible on factors you can control. The best way to influence the horse you cannot control is to focus on the one you can.

Thus, for example, when Anand Mahindra realized he needed to do something about the fact that outside analysts and large investors undervalued his conglomerate, he did not first rush out to try to change their minds. Instead, he had to consider that they were not just being arbitrary or unfair, that there were causes for their skepticism that he might be able to do something about. So he looked in the mirror at his own performance and then across the company's diverse divisions. He saw that he had failed to communicate a clear sense of purpose internally and, as a result, that the enterprise as a whole was neither coherent nor cohesive. He identified ways in which he could improve his performance in this area. Focusing on circumstances he could control, such as his own behavior, rather than those he could not—the behavior of analysts and investors—was the most effective way to begin changing the markets' perception of M&M.

Because of its inherent riskiness and uncertainty, Box 3 is an area in which it is essential to focus on controllable factors. The horse you can control in Box 3 is the process of disciplined experimentation that methodically tests propositions in order to increase knowledge and certainty. Not only does new knowledge enhance the prospects for control by resolving uncertainty, it can also expose otherwise hidden and potentially unruly circumstances that must be factored into future experiments.

With Scorpio, for example, M&M's shortage of new-vehicle engineering and design experience dictated the need to rely heavily on outside suppliers. Consequently, Scorpio's experiments in sourcing strategy were a way to test the extremely counterintuitive idea that M&M could better manage the car's development costs by extending to suppliers an unusually high level of trust and empowerment.[16] That, by itself, was a nonlinear process innovation, one that, moreover, created a feedback loop of new understanding transferred from suppliers to M&M's engineers.

Too often, an established mastery in executing a successful Box 1 business can feel like the pinnacle of control. You have developed and perfected the necessary internal skills and processes. You understand your customers and the market, having learned to anticipate and react to its rhythms, its ups and downs. And you have confidence, sometimes verging on arrogance, that you know what to do next. Soon enough, you are tempted to ride the obedient horse of Box 1 all the way through Box 2 and into Box 3 without stopping to consider what needs to be forgotten. You end up stuck in your comfort zone.

It's possible that M&M's most *comfortable* option for producing an original vehicle would have been to do it with Ford's assistance. But even Ford's chairman, Alex Trotman, understood this was a bad idea. It would have resulted in something that was neither new nor different, a vehicle "looking, smelling, and costing as much as a Ford."

Ultimately, to get to its future, M&M needed to escape its comfort zone. Instead, it opted for the exhilarating, motivating discomfort of a high-stakes Box 3 risk. The appropriate focus of control in Box 3 is driven by ignorance rather than complacency. There is so much you don't know yet about new customers, new technologies, new business models, and new types of risk. Consequently, you seek control through methodical investigation and discovery. Even within the adrenaline rush of its high-stakes gamble, the leaders of M&M's sourcing strategy were notably flexible and patient with suppliers. They sought to collaborate rather than dominate because listening and collaborating are the best ways to learn. And Box 3 is almost exclusively about committing to the process of learning.

Conclusion: Roots, Chains, and a Culture of Balance

During the years over which these events played out, the Mahindra Group developed a new way of seeing itself and devised a branding strategy that encapsulated the company's spirit in a single word: *rise*. Behind the word is a seventy-year-old story that connects the Mahindra Group founders' aspirations and values circa 1945 with a modern recognition of the ways the world and the company have changed since then.

Remarkably, however, elements of the Mahindra Group's original vision are preserved in today's "rise" formulation: to be a company that lifts up people and communities, setting no limits on what they can accomplish.[17]

As I mentioned in chapter 1, for organizations and people, it's helpful to think in terms of roots and chains. For a tree, roots sustain life. Cut the roots and the tree will die. Chains, on the other hand, create limits, constricting freedom of movement and threatening potential. Box 2 is where you must distinguish between roots and chains. Those critical distinctions ultimately reveal the aspects of your business that are timely and eventually perishable and those that are timeless and essential, and must be maintained. At the Mahindra Group, "rise" helped the company understand the differences between roots and chains.

"Rise" is a simple concept rooted in considerable thought and experience. Anand Mahindra used "rise" in guiding Box 2 decisions about the company's diverse portfolio of businesses, commenting, "Rise will increasingly become part of the portfolio logic. That's where a core purpose becomes extremely valuable. Rise businesses are those that allow you to do well and do good at the same time." For example, the Mahindra Group has a housing-finance unit that in part is helping make decent housing affordable to the growing middle classes of emerging markets. It is also the company's "fastest-growing business," according to Mahindra. Other so-called rise businesses invest in solar energy and agribusinesses and extend access to health insurance to markets where that concept is still relatively new.

On the other hand, the company may one day face rise-related portfolio decisions about defense-related businesses. In that context, said Mahindra, "at the very least, we have decided we are never going to make anything . . . that could be seen as offensive weaponry. We're never going to make explosive munitions." The company is, however, developing blast-resistant armor for vehicles manufactured for the military.

So you see how balance can become uniquely nuanced from one organization to the next, encompassing divergent sets of values, some with ethical dimensions, such as we have seen in Willow Creek, URI, Keurig, and other examples. In every enterprise, there will always be a need to distinguish roots from chains. Even in a relatively young organization like URI, which grew quickly through an acquisition strategy, we saw operational values being invented on the fly under CEO Mike Kneeland, board chair Jenne Britell, and other executives. In the hard work of reengineering Box 1, they built a discipline around treating employees with respect by being transparent and communicating clearly and honestly, even in difficult circumstances. That discipline will likely become part of the URI root system. But other things will reveal themselves in time as chains, just as Willow Creek learned when it saw the need to change the basic nature and purpose of its conferences.

As a leader, Anand Mahindra seems always to have had an instinct for balance. Whether it comes naturally or is learned the hard way, responsibility for creating a culture of balance, as well as ensuring the daily operational *fact* of balance, rests mainly with the CEO. Properly executing this discipline is a bit like being a doctor making morning rounds: it requires combining the ability to focus intensely on one patient's condition with an awareness that duty requires moving on to the next patient in a timely way. And just to extend the metaphor a bit further, because each patient is different, the doctor may need to adjust both style and method of treatment to achieve the best clinical outcome. The three boxes must be understood each on its own terms as well as in relation to the others.

This chapter and chapter 5 together provide a sort of narrative blueprint for balancing the three boxes. Creating the necessary culture requires combining structures, practices, and processes with the six essential leadership behaviors. Applied diligently and creatively, these ideas and different modes of approach will help you preserve the roots, break the chains, and build a sustainable future. This is the essence of the Three-Box Solution.

Takeaways

- *The six types of leadership behavior described in this chapter all contribute to achieving balance.* Bear in mind that they are not merely for occasional use under unusual circumstances. On the contrary, each one is part of the checklist of daily leadership responsibilities. To see them in any other way is to put a balanced Three-Box Solution at risk.

- *While each of the six behaviors is important in its own right, the practice of planned opportunism is paramount.* It has relevance in all three boxes and an overarching impact on the success of Three-Box Solutions. You cannot predict the future; you can only be ready for whatever it brings. If you can define and execute a portfolio of planned-opportunism initiatives for your organization, your Three-Box Solution is likely to thrive. The Mahindra story shows how planned opportunism played a key role in all three boxes, including changing the Box 1 culture.

- *When setting out to change a business culture, do not shy away from the hottest of hot-button issues.* Like Lou Gerstner trying to make IBM more customer focused, Anand Mahindra needed to fire "a rocket through the company" in order to shake it from its License Raj doldrums, so he took on the Diwali bonus. Doing the hardest things first can set the tone for everything that comes after.

- *Taking risks is underrated.* If your business is able to develop reasonable hedging strategies (such as a competency in frugal engineering and a phased strategy for investing in mavericks' ideas), it will be able to take risks more confidently. As Pawan Goenka noted about the Scorpio development project, nearly every aspect, including M&M's flexible, empowering approach to supplier relationships, was an experiment meant to produce learning that would make the big bet of the overall undertaking less risky.

- *There are many things you can do to minimize the impact of the horse you cannot control.* For example, URI sought to lessen its vulnerability to economic forces beyond its control by diversifying its customer base and deepening its relationships with large national accounts that helped it shift its business from more- to less-affected regions. Likewise, the Mahindra Group sought to improve its perceived value by more effectively communicating, articulating its purpose, and setting strategy across its divisions. These efforts made the company more coherent—both to itself and to the market—in ways that improved internal focus and market perceptions.

TOOLS

Tool 1: Where Does Your Organization's Culture Need Balance?

Reflect on the mind-sets and behaviors needed for Box 3 to succeed alongside a prosperous Box 1 business. Then take a clear-eyed look at your current company culture. What potentially limiting mind-sets and behaviors do you see that could get in the way of Box 3 success? How can you transform them by assembling a *dedicated team* empowered to pursue a "clean-slate" Box 2 approach? How will you mitigate cultural barriers or resistance instigated by the key stakeholders the dedicated team must rely on? What new cultural behaviors might you want to introduce across the organization to create harmony between Box 1 and Box 3 activities?

Tool 2: Assess Your Organization's Leaders (and Yourself)

One of the keys to three-box balance is the availability of leaders who can manage the three boxes well. How many in your organization possess the following traits? Evaluate a leader on the following dimensions using a 5-point scale, where 1 = totally disagree and 5 = totally agree. A total score of 27 or higher indicates an ambidextrous leader:

- Someone who can create the future while managing the present

- Someone able to operate comfortably in two time horizons (microscope *and* telescope)—one to three years as well as five to ten years

- Someone who is able to evaluate performance in a proven business model in an established industry as well as in a high-growth strategic experiment in an emerging industry

- Someone with the demonstrated ability to experiment, learn, and adapt as well as drive short-term financial performance

- Someone who can commit to embracing and leading change

- Someone able to leave behind behaviors, mind-sets, and attitudes that nonlinear changes have rendered obsolete

- Someone who understands the importance of placing smaller bets first, before placing bigger bets

- Someone able to detect inflection points and nonlinear shifts (weak signals) in the industry environment and know the appropriate time to initiate experiments to test new business models

- Someone who knows how to manage risk

How does your organization develop, retain, and reward leaders who are good in three-box balance?

Notes

Chapter 1

1. Michael L. Tushman and Charles A. O'Reilly III, *Winning Through Innovation: A Practical Guide to Leading Organizational Change and Renewal* (Boston: Harvard Business School Press, 2002).

2. C. K. Prahalad discussed weak signals as a way to unlock the future in an article by Art Kleiner, "The Life's Work of a Thought Leader," *strategy + business*, August 9, 2010.

3. Rebranded as Discovery Family Channel in October 2014.

Chapter 2

1. This and other events from Keurig's early days are described in a fascinating case by Paul W. Marshall and Jeremy B. Dann, "Keurig," HBS No. 899-180 (Boston: Harvard Business School Publishing, 1999 [revised 2004]). For the content in this chapter, I have drawn on published cases as well as on in-depth interviews with Dick Sweeney, John Whoriskey, and Kevin Sullivan.

2. Gillette innovated the legendary "razors and blades" business model that, by selling a relatively low-cost razor platform, created profitable future revenues from sales of the high-margin blades.

3. Marshall and Dann, "Keurig."

4. "A Progress Update from Bob Stiller (CEO) on Green Mountain's Investment in Keurig, Inc.," letter to stakeholders, May 15, 2003.

5. Nespresso, website fact sheet, http://www.nestle-nespresso.com/about-us/our-history.

6. By 2013, Nespresso had achieved just a 3 percent share of the US single-serve market. See http://www.bloomberg.com/news/articles/2014-02-19/nestle-supersizes-nespresso-for-u-s-coffee-drinkers.

Notes

7. Eric T. Anderson, "Keurig at Home: Managing a New Product Launch," Kellogg No. 105-005 (Evanston, IL: Northwestern University, Kellogg School of Management, 2005); this case includes detailed descriptions of Keurig's commissioned research, from which I have drawn for this sidebar.

8. Ibid.

9. Ibid.

10. Oliver Strand, "With Coffee, the Price of Individualism Can Be High," *New York Times*, February 7, 2012, http://www.nytimes.com/2012/02/08/dining/single-serve-coffee-brewers-make-convenience-costly.html?_r=0.

11. Elizabeth Gilbert, *Eat, Pray, Love: One Woman's Search for Everything Across Italy, India and Indonesia* (New York: Viking Press, 2006).

12. Ed Perratore, "Keurig 2.0 Pod Coffeemaker Rejects Older K-Cups," ConsumerReports.org, December 17, 2014, http://www.consumerreports.org/cro/news/2014/12/keurig-2-0-pod-coffeemaker-rejects-older-k-cups/index.htm.

13. Matt Krantz, "Keurig Mea Culpa: 'We Were Wrong,'" *USA Today*, May 8, 2015, http://americasmarkets.usatoday.com/2015/05/08/keurig-mea-culpa-we-were-wrong/.

14. Ibid.

15. Ibid.

16. Taryn Luna, "Keurig Bets on Cold-Brewing System to Heat Up Profits," *Boston Globe*, May 11, 2015.

Chapter 3

1. A variation of this story appears in Gary Hamel and C. K. Prahalad, *Competing for the Future* (Boston: HBS Press, 1996), 51.

2. "Jeff Immelt: A Simpler, More Valuable GE," announcement by chair and CEO, April 10, 2015, GE website, http://www.ge.com/stories/pivot.

3. S. Ramadorai, *The TCS Story . . . and Beyond* (India: Portfolio–Penguin Books, 2011).

4. Rachel Abrams, "P&G Sells 43 Beauty Brands to Coty," *New York Times*, July 9, 2015, http://www.nytimes.com/2015/07/10/business/dealbook/pg-sells-43-beauty-brands-to-coty.html?_r=0.

5. C. K. Prahalad coined the term "dominant logic." See Richard Bettis and C. K. Prahalad, "The Dominant Logic: Retrospective and Extension," *Strategic Management Journal* 16, no. 1 (1995): 5–14.

6. According to Moore's Law, the number of transistors in a dense integrated circuit doubles approximately every two years. Simply put, Moore's Law suggests that the cost of technology will keep declining, giving us the ability to build more-powerful computers at lower prices.

7. IBM competed on the basis of proprietary systems and protocols capable of interoperating only with other IBM systems, creating a high switching barrier.

8. Robert D. Austin and Richard L. Nolan, "IBM Corporation Turnaround," Case 600-098 (Boston: Harvard Business School Publishing, 2000).

9. Todd D. Jick and Mary C. Gentile, "Donna Dubinsky and Apple Computer, Inc. (A)," Case 486-083 (Boston: Harvard Business School Publishing, February 1986 [revised September 2011]).

10. Lynda M. Applegate, Robert D. Austin, and Elizabeth Collins, "IBM's Decade of Transformation: Turnaround to Growth," Case 805-130 (Boston: Harvard Business School Publishing, 2005 [revised 2009]).

11. Ibid.

12. Descriptions of the pervasive computing experience rely mainly on two sources: my conversations with Rodney Adkins, the leader of the pervasive computing unit, and a very useful case study by David A. Garvin and Lynne Levesque, "Emerging Business Opportunities at IBM (C): Pervasive Computing," Case 304-077 (Boston: Harvard Business School Publishing, 2004 [revised 2005]).

13. Garvin and Levesque, "Emerging Business Opportunities at IBM (C): Pervasive Computing," 6.

14. Ibid., 6.

15. Microsoft Corporation, "News Center," March 27, 2014, http://news.microsoft.com/2014/03/27/satya-nadella-mobile-first-cloud-first-press-briefing/.

16. Microsoft Corporation, "News Center," July 17, 2014, http://news.microsoft.com/2014/07/17/starting-to-evolve-our-organization-and-culture/.

17. Microsoft Corporation, "CEO," July 10, 2014, http://news.microsoft.com/ceo/bold-ambition/index.html.

18. Austin and Nolan, "IBM Corporation Turnaround."

19. Ibid.

20. Monica Langley, "Behind Ginni Rometty's Plan to Reboot IBM," *Wall Street Journal*, April 20, 2015, http://www.wsj.com/articles/behind-ginni-romettys-plan-to-reboot-ibm-1429577076.

21. Ibid.

22. Steve Lohr, "IBM Revenue Falls 13% Despite Big Gains in New Fields," *New York Times*, July 20, 2015, http://www.nytimes.com/2015/07/21/technology/-2015-07-21-technology-ibm-revenue-falls-13-percent-despite-big-gains-in-new-fieldshtml.html?_r=0.

Notes

Chapter 4

1. "United Rentals Announces Fourth Quarter and Full Year 2014 Results and Provides 2015 Outlook," United Rentals press release, January 21, 2015, http://www.unitedrentals.com/press-releases/2015/united-rentals-fourth-quarter-full-year-2014-results.pdf.

2. Jay W. Lorsch, Kathleen Durante, and Emily McTague, "United Rentals (A)," Case 414-043 (Boston: Harvard Business School Publishing, 2013).

3. In addition to Lorsch et al., "United Rentals (A)" and materials provided by Mike Kneeland and others at URI, this chapter relies on candid interviews with Kneeland, Jenne Britell, and Jeff Fenton.

Chapter 5

1. This and other aspects of the development of Willow Creek Community Church are described in Leonard A. Schlesinger and Jim Mellado, "Willow Creek Community Church (A)," Case 691-102 (Boston: Harvard Business School Publishing, 1991 [revised 1999]). For the Willow Creek content in this chapter, I have drawn on that case as well as on in-depth interviews with both Bill Hybels and Jim Mellado. Mellado, an evangelical Christian, later became president of the Willow Creek Association.

2. Schlesinger and Mellado, "Willow Creek Community Church (A)."

3. Ibid.

4. Ibid.

5. Ibid.

6. Ibid.

7. "A Holy Experiment," *Leadership Journal*, September 2014, http://www.christianitytoday.com/le/2014/september-online-only/holy-experiment.html?start=1.

8. Ibid.

9. Ibid.

10. Peter F. Drucker, "What Business Can Learn from Nonprofits," *Harvard Business Review*, July–August 1989.

11. Everett M. Rogers, *Diffusion of Innovations*, 5th ed. (New York: Free Press, August 2003).

12. S. Ramadorai, *The TCS Story ... and Beyond* (India: Portfolio–Penguin Books, 2011).

13. Ibid.

14. Ibid.

15. Ibid.

16. Ibid.

Chapter 6

1. Unless otherwise noted, material for this chapter relies on interviews with Anand Mahindra, chairman and managing director of the Mahindra Group, and Pawan Goenka, president of the Mahindra Group's automotive and farm equipment divisions.

2. "Commencement Address by Shri Anand Mahindra, Chairman and Managing Director, Mahindra & Mahindra," IIMA's 49th Annual Convocation, March 22, 2014, http://www.iimahd.ernet.in/assets/upload/events/1528538676Ch iefGuest-2014.pdf.

3. M&M's stock price underperformed the stock index. Investors no longer believed that M&M was a blue chip company. In January 2002, the Bombay Stock Exchange dropped M&M from the list of bellwether stocks that constituted Sensex.

4. Tarun Khanna, Rajiv Lal, and Merlina Manocaran, "Mahindra & Mahindra: Creating Scorpio," Case 705-478 (Boston: Harvard Business School Publishing, February 2005), 6.

5. Ibid.

6. Ketan Thakkar, "What Makes the Mahindra & Mahindra Cult Brand Scorpio Click," *Economic Times*, June 17, 2012.

7. Khanna et al., "Mahindra & Mahindra: Creating Scorpio," 8.

8. Ibid., 9.

9. Ibid., 9.

10. Ibid.

11. *Business Standard Motoring*, BBC World *Wheels*, and CNBC/Autocar all named the Scorpio 2003 "Car of the Year."

12. N. Madhavan, "How Mahindra & Mahindra Came to Dominate the Indian Automotive Industry," *Forbes India*, December 12, 2014.

13. Ibid.

14. Ibid.

15. Ibid.

16. This example shows that the uncontrollable horse doesn't always bring misfortune. For reasons beyond its control, the fortuitous timing of the Scorpio project made available to M&M many suppliers that were both skilled and eager for work. But M&M was able to leverage its availability to the highest degree by offering in return a uniquely collaborative partnership.

17. This is the company's core purpose: "We will challenge conventional thinking and innovatively use all our resources to drive positive change in the lives of our stakeholders and communities across the world, to enable them to Rise." Mahindra & Mahindra Ltd., "Who We Are: Our Purpose and Values," http://www.mahindra.com/Who-We-Are/Our-Purpose-and-Values.

Selected Bibliography

Anthony, Scott D., Mark W. Johnson, Joseph V. Sinfield, and Elizabeth J. Altman. *The Innovator's Guide to Growth: Putting Disruptive Innovation to Work*. Boston: Harvard Business Press, 2008.

Brown, Shona L., and Kathleen M. Eisenhardt. *Competing on the Edge*. Boston: Harvard Business School Press, 1998.

Christensen, Clayton M. *The Innovator's Dilemma*. Boston: Harvard Business Review Press, 1997.

Govindarajan, Vijay. "Designing a $300 House." *Harvard Business Review*, January–February 2011.

Govindarajan, Vijay. "A Reverse-Innovation Playbook." *Harvard Business Review*, April 2012.

Govindarajan, Vijay, and Ravi Ramamurti. "Delivering World-Class Health Care, Affordably." *Harvard Business Review*, November 2013.

Govindarajan, Vijay, and Chris Trimble. "Building Breakthrough Businesses Within Established Organizations." *Harvard Business Review*, May 2005.

Govindarajan, Vijay, and Chris Trimble. *Ten Rules for Strategic Innovators: From Idea to Execution*. Boston: Harvard Business Review Press, 2005.

Govindarajan, Vijay, and Chris Trimble. *The Other Side of Innovation: Solving the Execution Challenge*. Boston: Harvard Business Review Press, 2010.

Govindarajan, Vijay, and Chris Trimble. "Stop the Innovation Wars." *Harvard Business Review*, July–August 2010.

Govindarajan, Vijay, and Chris Trimble. "The CEO's Role in Business Model Reinvention." *Harvard Business Review*, January–February 2011.

Govindarajan, Vijay, and Chris Trimble. *Reverse Innovation: Create Far from Home, Win Everywhere*. Boston: Harvard Business Review Press, 2012.

Hamel, Gary, and C. K. Prahalad. *Competing for the Future*. Boston: Harvard Business School Press, 1996.

Selected Bibliography

Immelt, Jeffrey R., Vijay Govindarajan, and Chris Trimble. "How GE Is Disrupting Itself." *Harvard Business Review*, October 2009.

Kim, W. Chan, and Renée Mauborgne. *Blue Ocean Strategy*. Boston: Harvard Business School Press, 2005.

McGrath, Rita Gunther. *The End of Competitive Advantage*. Boston: Harvard Business Review Press, 2013.

Tushman, Michael L., and Charles A. O'Reilly III. *Winning Through Innovation*. Boston: Harvard Business School Press, 2002.

Winter, Amos, and Vijay Govindarajan. "Engineering Reverse Innovations." *Harvard Business Review*, July-August 2015.

Index

Index

Index

Index

Index

Index

Index

Acknowledgments

No one lives and works alone. I had the honor and privilege to present my ideas on the Three-Box Solution to more than five hundred thousand executives during the past thirty-five years. I am grateful for their help in shaping and refining my thinking. This book is as much theirs as it is mine.

I also would like to thank my family. Kirthi, my wife and best friend, has been both my most perceptive critic and my strongest defender. Her love has kept me going through the good times and the bad. My daughters, Tarunya and Pasy, are my hopes for the future. They read the manuscript pages and carried out this assignment with extraordinary efficiency and good humor. My sister Bama is all I could ask for in a sibling. I am deeply indebted to my family for their kindness, compassion, love, and so much more. Without their unfailing encouragement and support, the countless hours invested in this effort could not have come to fruition.

I could not have found a better adviser, ally, and friend than my editor at Harvard Business Review Press, Melinda Merino. I was also fortunate to have HBR contributing editor Lew McCreary draft the book. Lew's deft writing brings style, originality, charm, wit, and energy to these pages—far beyond what I could have achieved otherwise. Truly, without the two of them, this book would have not turned out so well. I am eternally grateful.

Finally, I would like to thank you for reading my book. My hope is that you can use the insights from *The Three-Box Solution* to lead innovation for the future while you maintain excellence in the present.

About the Author

Vijay Govindarajan (VG) is one of the world's leading experts on strategy and innovation. He is the author of twelve books and has published widely in academic and practitioner journals. His work has appeared on both the *New York Times* and the *Wall Street Journal* bestseller lists. Currently, he serves on both Dartmouth's and Harvard's faculty (the Coxe Distinguished Professor at the Tuck School of Business at Dartmouth College and a Marvin Bower Fellow at Harvard Business School).

During his career, VG has worked with the CEOs and top management teams of more than 25 percent of *Fortune* 500 firms to discuss, challenge, and deepen their thinking about strategy and innovation. He was the first Chief Innovation Consultant and Professor in Residence at General Electric. He worked with CEO Jeff Immelt to write "How GE Is Disrupting Itself," the *Harvard Business Review* article that pioneered the concept of "reverse innovation" (innovation adopted first by developing nations). HBR named reverse innovation one of the last century's "Great Moments in Management."

VG's research and teaching have garnered numerous accolades. He was inducted into the *Academy of Management Journal*'s Hall of Fame and was ranked by *Management International Review* as one of the Top-20 North American Superstars for research in strategy. In the latest Thinkers50 rankings, VG is rated the number one Indian

Management Thinker. Much in demand on the lecture circuit, he has been a keynote speaker in the *BusinessWeek* CEO Forum, HSM World Business Forum, TED, and the World Economic Forum at Davos.

Prior to joining the faculty at Tuck, he served on the faculties of Harvard Business School, INSEAD (Fontainebleau), and the Indian Institute of Management in Ahmedabad, India. VG received both his doctorate and MBA (with distinction) from Harvard Business School.

VG and his wife, Kirthi, divide their time between Hanover, New Hampshire, and Boston, Massachusetts.